ART&DESIGN

ACADEMY GROUP LTD
42 LEINSTER GARDENS, LONDON W2 3AN
TEL: 0171-262 5097 FAX: 0171-262 5093

EDITOR: Nicola Kearton
PRODUCTION EDITOR: Ramona Khambatta
ART EDITOR: Alex Young
DESIGN: Artmedia

SUBSCRIPTION OFFICES:
UK:JOHN WILEY & SONS LTD
JOURNALS ADMINISTRATION DEPARTMENT
1 OLDLANDS WAY, BOGNOR REGIS
WEST SUSSEX, PO22 9SA, UK
TEL: 01243 843272; FAX: 01243 843232
E-MAIL: cs journals@wiley.co.uk

USA AND CANADA: JOHN WILEY & SONS, INC
JOURNALS ADMINISTRATION DEPARTMENT
695 THIRD AVENUE
NEW YORK, NY 10158, USA
TEL: 212 850 6645 FAX: 212 850 6021
E-MAIL: subinfo@jwiley.com

ALL OTHER COUNTRIES:
VCH VERLAGSGESELLSCHAFT MBH
POSTFACH 101161
69451 WEINHEIM, GERMANY
TEL: 00 49 6201 606 148 FAX: 00 49 6201 606 117

CONTENTS

ART & DESIGN **MAGAZINE**

'Earthly Delight' • *Academy Highlights*

ART & DESIGN **PROFILE** *No 57*

ART & THE GARDEN

TRAVELS IN THE CONTEMPORARY MINDSCAPE

Guest-edited by Anne de Charmant

ARCHITECTURAL DESIGN PROFILE NO 130
CONTEMPORARY MUSEUMS

Museums, as they have emerged in the 1990s are a heady mixture of, what Charles Jencks calls, 'culture and speculation, spirituality and glamour, self-improvement and power'. They have become recognised as a potent new building type which must combine the seemingly contradictory tasks of Cathedral and Shopping Mall as well as the traditional roles of preserving, interpreting and memorialising artefacts and events. *Architectural Design* looks at the connection between commerce and the new museum exploring how architects are responding to requirements? The issue debates whether museums and art galleries are solely designed for displaying art and artifacts for commercial gain, how much they reaffirm establishment values, are they the religious centres of the generation? As Andreas Huyssen puts it, the prevalence of museum building today could be a deep psychological response to the ephemeralisation of life by the media. Projects featured include Richard Meier's Museum of Television and Radio, Los Angeles; Norman Foster's American Air Museum, Duxford, Britain; Hans Hollein's Guggenheim Museum, Vienna; Frans Hak's Groninger Museum, The Netherlands; Kisho Kurokawa's Shiga Kogen Roman Art Museum, Nagano, Japan. Extracts from the proceedings of the symposium 'Spectacular Contradictions: Museums in the 1990s' at the Royal Academy of Arts in June 1996 will also be included along with essays by Charles Jencks, Nicholas Serota and Clare Melhuish.

PB 0-471-977381 £18.95 $32.50
305x250 mm, 112 pages
Illustrated throughout
November 1997

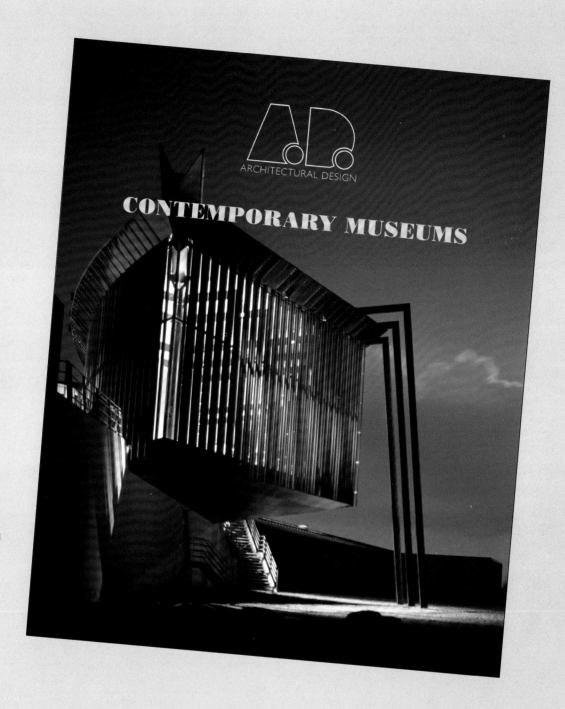

Further information can be obtained from:
(UK only) Academy Group Ltd, 42 Leinster Gardens, London W2 3AN. Tel: 0171 402 2141 Fax: 0171 723 9540

(USA and Canada) National Book Network, 4720 Boston Way, Lanham, Maryland 20706, USA
Tel: (301) 459 3366 Fax: (301) 459 2118

(Rest of World) VCH, Postfach 101161, 69451 Weinheim, Federal Republic of Germany
Tel: +49 6201 606 144 Fax: +49 6201 606 184

Daphne Wright, Lot's Wife, 1996, wire and tin foil with soundtrack

Jefford Horrigan, Carbon Garden (left), Viral Garden (right), 1997, oil on canvas

Elizabeth Jane Grose, Park, 1996, approx 1,500 translucent pigmented resin casts of toy cars (foreground); Edwina Fitzpatrick, After Eden: Pedigree, 1997 (background), apple tree (Malus sylvestris, also commonly known as Eden's 'tree of knowledge'); scientific equipment (laboratory test tubes and clamps); mould (created in non-sterile environments); micro-propagation fluid (a highly fertile mixture, commonly found in horticultural laboratories to make clones of plant cuttings – as used with seedless grapes); apple seeds (carrying the DNA of both parent plants – as used in nature); family trees (the genetic line of the House of Windsor since George V – see text); text (the rulers of England and their pedigrees).

All shown at Burford House Gallery, Shropshire

EARTHLY DELIGHT

At a time when the Western world has few remaining wild places, we have become very nostalgic, even sentimental, about nature. Perhaps this begins to explain our enjoyment of the garden. We hanker for our own little piece of Eden, trying to return to something lost to us. Yet even here we desire perfection and control, coercing wayward nature into an ideal form which bears little resemblance to unmanaged landscape. By growing tropical plants in temperate climates, or by trying to produce ever brighter blooms and stronger, sweeter scents, some 'desirable' aspects of nature are encouraged, whilst others are suppressed. Torn between delight in the untamed and the urge to colonise its chaos, in the garden we are forced to consider the construct of Nature and where we position ourselves within it.

For 'Earthly Delight' four artists were invited to present works which use the garden as a means of re-assessing our complex contemporary relationship with the natural. The collision of nature and culture, the intoxicating fiction of the garden as a natural idyll, and the manipulation of nature are amongst the ideas they explore.

Why should it be that some elements of nature are thought to be beautiful or decorative, whilst others are not? Stylised images of plants as ornament in architecture and interiors are perennially popular, and seeking even to enhance nature's own creations, we populate our gardens with hybrids. In Jefford Horrigan's paintings, scientific diagrams of the structures of chemicals or viruses masquerade as designs for topiary and box hedging. Sprouting from chromosome-shaped roots, his sculptures for walls and ceilings bring to mind the fleshy, pungently scented 'parodies of nature' which enchanted Huysman's Des Esseintes in À rebours. Human appropriation and manipulation reaches beyond the cosmetic into fundamental structures and systems.

Elizabeth Jane Grose's *Park* takes the Italianate Gardens in Regent's Park as a starting point for thinking about contemporary ambivalence towards nature. Whilst it might be read as forewarning of environmental disaster, substituting each plant with a miniature car cast in jewel-bright resin, *Park* seems also to proffer an alternative to the organic garden. The related series of drawings further problematises the notion of the natural as inherently pure and desirable, hinting that a flower, observed, named, planted, pruned, is as much a cultural product as a car.

The expulsion from Eden and its aftermath, humankind's mythological separation from nature, is central to Edwina Fitzpatrick's new work *Pedigree*. The line of accession of the Royal House of Windsor has been marked out with a complex, yet sensuous, system of text-tubes and pipes. A living, fruiting apple tree grows against the opposite wall. The pipes contain a micropropagation fluid, which will support and nourish the apple pips planted inside. This technique is usually employed in the sterile environment of the laboratory to clone plants from cuttings, bypassing nature's reproductive systems. Fitzpatrick has harnessed the processes of germination, growth and decay, to draw our attention to the systems of inherited power and wealth which shape and control our society.

Daphne Wright's installations play upon ideas about reality and artifice, using an uncompromisingly banal and barren material to embody an idea of the natural. In *Lot's Wife*, an orchard of silver pear trees, crafted from tin foil, springs from concrete blocks. Our nostalgia for nature ensures that at first glimpse the orchard appears exquisite, luxuriant. It soon becomes clear that the orchard is the product of a blighted nature, bewitched like the petrified garden of a fairytale. Eerie, cold and lifeless the slender tree trunks are bowed by the weight of an implausibly heavy harvest. None of the fruits seem edible – some are grotesquely overblown, the rest are small, looking as if they could never ripen. An old man's voice whispers 'April Fool' chiding the viewer for being seduced by the orchard's superficial prettiness. The title serves perhaps as another reminder about the dangers of looking back.
Maria Brewster, Curator

'Earthly Delight' is a collaborative exhibition and education project organised by Ikon Touring, Birmingham, Burford House Gallery, Shropshire and The Teulon Cottage, Birmingham Botanical Gardens and Glasshouses.

Acknowledgements

We have borrowed and freely interpreted the term 'mindscape', in the subtitle, from Günter Nitschke who first used it in his book *Japanese Gardens*. Anne de Charmant would like to thank Charles Chesshire, Simon Cutts, Romain Lacroix and Patrick Sabatier for their help in preparing this issue. *Art & Design* would like to thank Anne de Charmant for her work in compiling this issue along with all the contributors and their galleries for generous contributions. We are also grateful to Vivian Constantinopoulos and Robert Anderson for their translations. All material is courtesy of the following artists and galleries:

p1: Michel Desvigne; **Gardens Past and Present** *pp2-5: pp4-5* photo Clive Nichols, with thanks to Christopher Bradley-Hole; **Monumental Monochrome Landscape Generator** *pp10-11: p11* Burattoni & Abrioux; **The Power of Beauty** *pp12-15: pp14-15* Metro Pictures, New York; **Plants and Design** *pp16-19:* Charles Chesshire; **The Universe as Measure** *pp20-29:* Charles Jencks; **Theatre Garden** *pp30-33:* Translated by Robert Anderson, images Rüdiger Schöttle; **Changing the Myth** *pp34-39:* Gilles Clément, Atelier Acanthe, Paris; **Japanese Contemporary Gardens** *pp40-47: p40, pp42-43, pp46-47;* Günter Nitschke; **Derek Jarman's Garden** *pp48-53:* The author would like to thank Keith Collins for his help and encouragement with this piece, photos Gillian Watson; **Chaumont** *pp54-57:* Festival International des Jardins de Chaumont sur Loire; **Future Garden** *pp58-59:* Kunst-und Ausstellungshalle der Bundesrepublik Deutschland; **From Land Art to Garden Landscape** *pp60-65: p60, p62 centre and below* Bernard Lassus; *p62 above* Annely Juda Fine Art, London, *p64* Anthony d'Offay Gallery, London; **The Little Spartan Wars** *pp66-67:* John Stathatos; **The Renewal of French Gardening** *pp76-81:* Translated by Vivian Constantinopoulos, images *p77* Bernard Lassus, *pp78-79* Parc de la Villette, Paris, *p80* Michel Desvigne, *p81* Pascal Cribier; **Beyond Eden** *pp82-87:* Translated by Robert Anderson, images *pp84-86* Susanne Prinz, *p87* Fondation Cartier pour l'Art Contemporain, Paris; **Nature Works** *pp88-92* Meg Webster, *p88, p92* Morris Healy Gallery, New York.

Contributors' Biographies

Anne de Charmant is a writer and curator based in London, she is a correspondent for *Muséart* and *Tate* magazine and is also Director of Burford House Gallery, Shropshire. **Yves Abrioux** is a writer and landscape historian who lives and works outside Paris. Since 1994, he and the Paris-based artist **Gianni Burattoni** have embarked on a series of collaborations under the generic title 'Essays in the Landscape'. **Ronald Jones** is an artist based in New York. He is also Chair of the Visual Arts Division and the Director of the Digital Media Lab at Columbia University in New York City. He is represented by Metro Pictures and the Sonnabend Gallery, New York. **Charles Chesshire** is a landscape and garden designer currently Curator of Burford House Gardens. Also a writer he is currently working on two publications for the RHS/Dorling Kindersley. **Charles Jencks** is an architectural critic, the author of *The Jumping Universe, The Language of Post-Modern Architecture* and *Architecture Today*, all published by Academy Editions as well as many other books on contemporary building and Post-Modern thought. **Rüdiger Schöttle** has had a gallery in Munich since 1968. His publications include *Psychomachia* (1990) and *Bestiarium der Kunst, Texte im Bilderlabyrinth* (1995). **Gilles Clément** is a landscape and garden designer based in Paris, he designed the gardens of the Domaine Rayol and co-designed the Parc André Citröen. He teaches at the Ecole d'Architecture de Versailles and at the Ecole Nationale Supérieure du Paysage. His most influential publications are *Le jardin en mouvement* (1994) and *Libres jardins* (1997). **Günter Nitschke** is Director of the Institute for East Asian Architecture and Urbanism, he has lectured worldwide and is an authority on Japanese gardens, recent books include *Japanese Gardens* (1991) and *The Silent Orgasm* (1995). **Stephanie Watson** is a writer and researcher who works on issues of gender/identity and cultural theory. **Helen Mayer Harrison** and **Newton Harrison** are artists and have been exhibiting together for over 30 years. They shared a professorship at the University of California at San Diego in La Jolla and each of them individually headed the Department of Visual Arts. They are represented by Ronald Feldman in New York. **Stephen Bann** is Professor of Modern Cultural Studies, University of Kent and his most recent publication is *Paul Delaroche: History Painted* (1997). **John Stathatos** is a photo-based artist, writer and curator. He edits the arts magazine *Untitled* and guest-edited A&D *Art & the City: A Dream of Urbanity* No 50. **Jean-Pierre Le Dantec** is President and Professor at the Ecole d'Architecture de Paris La Villette. His most influential publications are *Dédale le héro* (1982), *Jardin et paysage* (1996) and *Reading the French Garden* (1991). **Susanne Prinz** is an art historian, writer and curator based in Berlin. She is currently preparing a show called 'It's a small world' for the Berliner Ensemble. **Meg Webster** is an artist based in New York.

COVER: Bernard Lassus, Les Buissons Optiques, Niort, 1993
INSIDE COVERS: Helen Mayer Harrison, Newton Harrison, Future Garden: Part I, 1996-98, Kunst-und Ausstellungshalle der Bundesrepublik, Deutschland, Bonn, photo Peter Oszvald

EDITOR: Nicola Kearton   PRODUCTION EDITOR: Ramona Khambatta
ART EDITOR: Alex Young   DESIGN: Artmedia

First published in Great Britain in 1997 by *Art & Design* an imprint of
ACADEMY GROUP LTD

Art & Design Profile 57 is published as part of *Art & Design* Vol 12 11/12 1997
Art & Design Magazine is published six times a year and is available by subscription

Other Wiley Editorial Offices
New York • Weinheim • Brisbane • Singapore • Toronto

Distributed to the trade in the United States of America by
NATIONAL BOOK NETWORK, INC, 4720 BOSTON WAY, LANHAM, MARYLAND 20706

ISBN 0-471-97745-4

Printed and bound in Italy

Art & Design

ART & THE GARDEN
TRAVELS IN THE CONTEMPORARY MINDSCAPE

*Michel Desvigne, public space in front of the Hôtel du Module d'Echange,
1997, Roissy Charles de Gaule Airport, Paris (architect Paul Andreu)*

ACADEMY EDITIONS • LONDON

GARDENS PRESENT AND FUTURE
ANNE DE CHARMANT

In the beginning was the Garden; Garden of Eden or of the Hesperides, Pardes of the Kabbala or Paradise on Earth from which man and woman were banished. The garden has always been the precious space where man situates his utopias, collecting there the best of creation and the highest designs in an attempt to shape his vision of paradise. What this paradise presumes to be and which utopia is illustrated is however a changeable matter and has given rise to many lost masterpieces from Egypt to Rome and from Persia to China. Whether a representation of the sacred, of power, of memory or even of fantasy, the garden is the place of culture and art *par excellence*.

In this century however the concept of the garden and gardens themselves have undergone radical mutations. Following urban and industrial developments, pleasure gardens – replacing once and for all the utilitarian enclosure – have multiplied rapidly and become immensely accessible. The act of gardening itself has emerged as one the most favoured leisure activities, revealing a deep craving to celebrate the gifts of a Nature that was otherwise being sacrificed. And more prosaically creating a whole new thriving economic and media sector.

In celebrating this private ritual however, the broader intent and more symbolic language of the garden was effectively being lost, buried 'down the garden path', drowned in the colourful mixed border of a jubilant horticultural diversity. In the process, did the garden lose its focus and edge as a language and an artform? As Robert Smithson asked in 1968, 'Could one say that art degenerates as it approaches gardening?'. And how can we read and assimilate such heritages as the picturesque and land art today? Remembering and repositioning a number of essential questions about the landscape and the garden that have fashioned our understanding, Yves Abrioux attempts to define a fictional new criterion: the 'gardenesque' (no relation to Loudon's 1830s terminology).

One 'culprit' for this horticultural debauchery is the passion for newly discovered or newly manufactured plants that has gradually taken hold of the gardeners of this world and drawn all their energies. Charles Chesshire reviews the principal stages of this evolution whereby plants, from being the media of an artform, have often become objets d'art in themselves. And nowhere is this more true than in Britain where this horticultural passion has reached peaks of excellence. As a result, garden design is often regarded as a mere showcase in which to parade a wealth of blooms and its symbolic language has become overridden by a superficial grammar of cliches. From the strong propositions of a few great gardeners at the end of the 19th century and in the first half of the 20th, a window-dressing vocabulary of ponds and paths, borders and hedges has emerged that seems to satisfy all and serve all purposes. However well crafted and immediately pleasing some of these schemes might be, they purport to a brand of design that, widely customised and publicised through a myriad of magazines or television programmes, is in many ways responsible for an impoverishment of a major artform.

It is now however, in the dawn of the 21st century, that we need this language most. Our relation to a new global and mutating environment is more precarious and complex than ever but in the space of the garden it has a chance of being laid out and expressed perhaps more penetratingly than anywhere else. How else could one explain the current fascination of artists with gardens, landscape and the natural media? This attraction, as well the cross fertilisation or osmosis between art and landscape design, is examined from different angles in this issue of *Art & Design*. Stephen Bann endeavours to clarify the notions of land art, differentiate the concept of the sculpture park and define the garden as an artform in itself. On the other hand, Ronald Jones, a theoretician himself and artist, points to the contradictions and crippling self-consciousness that can arise from landscape design aspiring to the 'higher' status of art. The pursuit of a response to changing times that would elevate them to the level of the contemporary art 'aristocracy', often ends with designers or landscape architects leaving out the fundamental constituent of their art: the sense of beauty and place.

It is a fact that if 'modern' or contemporary garden design is frequently derided and denounced it is often due to the superficial and hollow assimilation of elements of modernist architecture, oriental abstraction or so-called contemporary materials. But overwhelmingly it is due to the fact that the global understanding and practice of gardens today still favours the recreation of a standardised 'romantic' vision based on a determined bank of images. Maybe more than in any other areas of the arts, the 'masterpiece' gardens of the past hold a powerful spell. Nowhere is this more true than in Britain where tremendous efforts and financial means are devoted to recreating or restoring schemes of the past while hardly any substantial new creation has emerged. There are of course some isolated attempts within major events and a few platforms for the promotion of the contemporary art of the garden but no visible

OVERLEAF: Christopher Bradley-Hole, The Latin Garden, 1997, presented by the Daily Telegraph and American Express at the Chelsea Flower Show, London. This rigorously modern garden of streamlined stonework, glass and steel with Mediterranean-style planting draws its inspiration from the poetry of antiquity and the life of the Roman poet, Virgil. (photo Clive Nichols)

movement or important realisation has actually broken the surface of the traditional 'garden world'. Even the contemporary arts, apart from the creation of important sculpture parks and the initiative of individual artists, seem confined to the gallery and museum, thereby hindering dialogue and cross fertilisation. This is not the case in Germany where a multitude of contemporary public gardens has recently been created which, as Susanne Prinz determines, takes on crucial questions relating to identity and memory. In Japan, where gardens that could be identified as abstract or conceptual by a Western eye were created in the 14th or 15th centuries, designers and artists also find new directions for establishing man's changing relationship to nature. France, over the past decades, has seen the emergence of enormous public interest in contemporary gardens with the success of such public realisations as La Villette and the Parc André Citroën in Paris. This sanctions an incredibly vital scene of the art of the garden mapped out here by Jean-Pierre Le Dantec. The Festival des Jardins de Chaumont-sur-Loire which describes itself as a laboratory for the 21st century garden is another very successful avatar of this revival.

This is a striking contrast with the designer's gardens of the Chelsea Flower Show where year after year – and with a few exceptions – variations on the same theme are presented albeit in the most magnificent manner. Although one must mention the distinction of Christopher Bradley-Hole's 'Latin' garden in 1997 as all round winner and the previous distinction of such designers as Dan Pearson which might herald a profound change. But for the time being, the situation in Britain is such that architects such as Sir Richard Rogers or Sir Norman Foster call upon the French designer Alain Provost to landscape major projects like the Greenwich riverside gardens and the Westminster–Trafalgar Square area. They apparently do not find the appropriate forces in this country to deal with the demands of a modern or urbanistic context. The Tate found itself in the same position when it came to commissioning the future gardens of the new Gallery of Modern Art at Bankside. After trying to find the talent in Britain they finally commissioned the Swiss landscape firm of Kienast Vogt.

But despite all a craving to change references does exist in Britain which sometimes comes to the fore. As proof, the recent major public success of a publication on the late Derek Jarman's garden in Dungeness which Stephanie Watson revisited. There the English ideal and tradition of the garden is dissolved and sublimated through an exercise in honesty and poetry. Also referring penetratingly to a classical tradition is Ian Hamilton Finlay's masterpiece of Little Sparta at Stonypath. One of the issues this highly influential garden unearths is the question of the status of a place as sacred and unique as a garden. John Stathatos chronicles the legal battle between Hamilton Finlay and the Scottish local authorities. As well as exploring a cultural map as does Little Sparta, a garden can be an instrument of wisdom in a more scientific sense. Charles Jencks has found in the art of the garden a language which places him, 'in a palpable relationship with the universe' and he is continuing work on the 'garden of cosmic speculation'.

Beyond the coded constraints of such categories as land art, earth works, installation or environmental art – none of which form the subject of this issue – it seems that artists who choose to use the garden, experience a total freedom. The eclectic choice of artists represented in this volume mirrors this state of affairs. They are not 'garden artists' but individuals who temporarily, incidentally, or more permanently, find in the garden a privileged mode of expression – whether they choose to use it as a medium, as a referential tool or as an ecological system. It is ultimately of little importance whether the artist works with actual plantings like Meg Webster – who must take into account such considerations as the evolution of her work in terms of growth and maintenance – or whether they do not even refer to the living media – like Rüdiger Schöttle who evolved his Theatre Garden purely as a symbolic model exploring the culture from which it stems.

For artists and so-called designers alike, ecological awareness in all its forms (ideological, scientific or political) has enduringly and profoundly marked the reflection on the natural or cultural site. But for some more than others, using nature as a media and evolving cogent systems from our environment is a act that goes beyond art. The French garden designer Gilles Clément's reflection on our relationship to wilderness and the model of the jardin en mouvement which he evolved, takes on broadly the same issues as Helen Mayer Harrison and Newton Harrison, the American artists who have been working for decades with defined eco-systems and cultural landscapes such as the endangered meadows. Clément has taken his reflection beyond the conventional boundaries of the garden to evolve the concept of the planetary garden, with man tending it as a responsible and committed gardener, while the Harrisons see the meadow as a metaphor of an old wisdom and a model for a Future Garden that could spread over continents.

NOTES TOWARDS A DEFINITION OF THE GARDENESQUE
YVES ABRIOUX

Could one say that art degenerates as it approaches gardening? (Robert Smithson, 1968)

For a while (in my experience) I was greatly perplexed as to why Stonypath did not have a garden-y garden. (Ian Hamilton Finlay, 1971)

There is perhaps no starker way of approaching the status of the garden in contemporary art than via the opposition between American earth works and the poetic and painterly tradition of the English garden.

Ian Hamilton Finlay's notion and experience of gardens and gardening colours his entire artistic output. Not only has he stated that his interest in the French Revolution stemmed from the difficulties he encountered in establishing the garden at Stonypath; the problem of the transmutation of a site into a garden, in the full sense of the word, parallels the familiar but historically inextricable difficulties involved in fulfilling a revolutionary process. When can a revolution be considered to have been successfully completed? When can a garden be said to be garden-y?

Gardens are a matter of culture – literally and in all senses.

Alone perhaps among American artists of his generation evolving within the domain of land art, Robert Smithson displayed an interest in and an understanding of the picturesque.

With its roots in 18th-century cultural tourism, the picturesque is not in any straightforward sense an aesthetics of painting or drawing.

What I propose to call the gardenesque will not simply be an aesthetics of gardening.

The picturesque promoted the mobilisation of a painterly sensibility as an aid to the appreciation of the environment. It could take an explicitly practical form, as in the use of the Claude glass. Although it induced a vast corpus of travel literature, the picturesque largely reduced the landscape to muteness.

Eighteenth-century landowners derived from the picturesque real and imaginative vantage points from which to read views of their estates in painterly terms. Agricultural workers could thus be seen rather than heard, the 'dark' side of the agricultural landscape was aestheticised, relations of power and property were masked.

Eighteenth-century travellers made their way across lands in which the highly visible property relations of feudalism were changing and in which the unproductive, threatening edges of the cultivated and cultured world that had long been perceived as the dustbins of Creation – ie the sea and mountains – were only just beginning to come into civilised view. (As late as 1796, the young Hegel was careful to turn his gaze away from the horror of Alpine summits during a walking tour of Switzerland.) The picturesque provided early tourists with a means of accommodating the eye and the imagination to strange or estranged topographical and social environments.

The explorers, who in Europe's name were at the same time laying claim to the furthest reaches of the globe, produced a literature of more obvious cognitive value than that of most picturesque tourists. They too, however, mobilised the conventions of landscape painting – in word or with pencil or brush, and indeed on the ground – in order to familiarise (colonise) supposedly savage tracts of land. Landscape, suggests WJT Mitchell, 'is a medium found in all cultures' but it is also 'a particular historical formation associated with European imperialism'.

The same may be said of gardens. The fact that the great gardens of empire did without (visible) walls is indicative of a particular mode of inscription in the national or international environment. Seen from the palace windows, Le Nôtre's garden at Versailles – which exploits, at the heart of France, the technology used by Vauban for the fortifications he was erecting to guard the kingdom's frontier – extends in orderly degrees towards the untutored landscape in the distance. In a metaphorical rather than metonymic mode, the English landscape garden established a landlord's more or less fictional relations of filiation and rights of occupation; it engaged imaginatively in national politics and contributed to the continental war effort.

Coined by John Claudius Loudon in the 1830s, the term 'gardenesque' referred to a *style* of gardening that highlighted individual trees and shrubs, whereas the picturesque had privileged clumps and overall effects. Furthermore, whereas the picturesque had inscribed (or disguised) manifestly cultural ambitions within its wider landscape effects, the gardenesque was suburban in scope and botanical in its interests.

The gardenesque, as I propose to use the term, does not share Loudon's bias. It does not operate a restriction of the picturesque in scale and in portent. Rather, in a gesture of homage to the *logic* of the picturesque, it proposes to mobilise a sensibility attuned to gardens – understood as a historically significant cultural manifestation – as an adjunct to the consideration of the visual arts.

The gardenesque is to the picturesque what *ektopias* (texts translated into landscapes) might be to *ekprasis* (pictures translated into texts).

Lucius Burkhardt's *promenadologie* is a 'science' of walking or touring which may, for example, involve experimentally confronting the 18th-century literature of exploration with all too familiar sites of contemporary urban alienation, in order to produce a practical experience of the uncanny.

Gardens and the gardenesque may similarly de-familiarise our surroundings.

Michel Foucault classes gardens amongst what he calls *heterotopias*: institutionally sanctioned 'other spaces' which represent but also contest and invert modes of societal and cultural placement.

Garden are spaces at once material and imaginary. Traditionally, they have offered proleptic and/or analeptic visions of an ideal order.

The ancient tradition of walled 'paradise' gardens sought to carve out the ideal in hostile surroundings from which it had to be protected.

In the stable world of the metaphysical or religious *empirium*, gardens were able to function as theatres of memory – literally, even, in the sense enshrined in the age-old 'art of memory' which in the course of time acquired a cosmological resonance.

The Renaissance evolved, by way of Cicero, the notion of a 'third nature'. Following on from the 'primary' wilderness and the 'secondary nature' fashioned by human settlement and the exploitation of resources, this characterised the status of gardens which were held to represent, and indeed epitomise, the order implicit in the other two natures.

The crisis of representation occurred in gardens two centuries earlier than in the visual arts, when English landscape gardeners resolved to outdo classical models and make the Ancients speak good English. (In between times, German Romanticism had gone through a similar process with respect to the authority of classical French culture.)

The end-point of the English landscape garden was a mode of self-representation in which parks and their surroundings came to epitomise the quintessential 'colour' of England. It consequently became easy to claim that the disappearance of overt signs of art represented the triumph of nature over artifice.

The landscapes fashioned by 'Capability' Brown were to be as indistinguishable from their topographical surroundings as today's art after the 'end' of art can be from the sociocultural environment, which, even if it no longer poses as 'anti-'art with the same degree of militancy, it may imitate to the point of being absorbed into its processes and rituals. In either case, artifice proceeds by camouflaging itself.

Whatever the reality of contemporary gardening practice or the renewed interest in gardening history and the poetics of gardens, the current prevalence of the notion of 'landscape architecture' reinforces the (temporary?) demise of the garden as a significant concept in art.

The gardenesque, in contrast, suggests regarding the art of gardening as having perhaps been displaced towards other sites in our culture.

It does not suggest that art should necessarily 'approach gardening' in any literal sense.

It does not concern itself with so-called 'sculpture parks' in which art works are put out to grass. Almost by definition, such places miss out on the problematical disappearance – in theory more than in practice – of the garden as art.

The gardenesque argues that a sense of what gardens are or were – of their scale and their particular station in the environment, of their history beyond their proclaimed absorption into nature – provides a valuable, and if necessary polemical, approach to certain aspects of contemporary art.

As a criterion rather than a category, the gardenesque proposes considering typical manifestations of contemporary art as if they were notional gardens – not in order to suggest a new system of classification but as a measure of the strengths and weaknesses of the works in question.

Is the principle of *site-specific art* not potentially a debilitating reversal of the 18th-century suggestion that landscape gardeners should develop the 'capabilities' of a given site?

What insights might one derive from regarding *installation art* as a variation on the poetics of gardening? It is true that installations are more often than not temporary; they are typically created out of urban and/or technological materials.

Nevertheless, they impinge – as all significant gardens also do – on the articulation between a self-contained environment and its immediate or more distant (physical, social, cultural, historical, etc) contexts. They solicit both eye and bodily movement – sometimes in the contradictory manner of the picturesque garden, which strove to prevent the stroller's eye and footsteps from ever following an identical line. Installations also play on the tension between imaginary dimensions and the constraints of collective space, both physical and conventional.

Is the problem with much *land art* not that it typically constructs or places a sculptural form on or near the surface of the globe, in such a way that it will hopefully function on a planetary scale, or indeed that it will plug into cosmological forces? Even putting aside the ideological reservations inspired by the dependence of such a project on a post-romantic philosophy of nature, it must be pointed out that, in striving for a frequently spurious late-modern sublime, it misses out on the difficult human scale.

Robert Smithson's objection to the gardenesque stems from the perception that gardens 'tame' wildness and that the picturesque ruins of the English landscape-garden tradition nostalgically project the dream of pastoral harmony into the pre-industrial past. The artist, however, corrects this critique in a footnote. Observing that 'Dreadful things seem to have happened in those half-forgotten Edens', with the result that 'Too much thinking about "gardens" leads to perplexity and agitation', he recognises that 'The abysmal problem of gardens somehow involves a fall from somewhere or something. The certainty of the absolute garden will never be regained'.

The Edenic tradition of gardens meets the assuaging tendencies of art in what Panofsky, deliberately misreading the Latin tag in Poussin's painting of Arcadian shepherds, calls the 'elegiac tradition' of *Et in Arcadia Ego*. The shepherds' silent deciphering of the monitory inscription in Poussin's painting is thus held to mark an interiorisation of its message, which transforms the bluntness of a *momento mori* into a stimulus for a cosmological meditation gently rocked by the recurring cycle of the seasons.

Ian Hamilton Finlay's 'footnote' to this tradition injects the iconography of modern warfare into the garden, exploding the logic of melancholy and solace. His literal citations of terror reinsert the grammatically correct reading (as opposed to the shadow of a departed friend) into Arcadia, hyperbolically challenging the status of gardens in history and culture.

On a different scale, Smithson's *non-sites* abstractly question the power of any enclosure – and therefore notionally of gardens – to arrest the process of 'necessity and chance' which the artist associates with geological time and with entropy. However, Smithson also observes that the texture of the picturesque garden 'dialectically' responds to the challenge of a temporal process exceeding the illusory constraints of the 'formal ideal'.

The gardenesque is a form of realism which follows up signs of such a contradictory sensibility even where this avoids the mode of the sublime.

It strives to disseminate the tensions historically implicit in gardens throughout our culture.

The gardenesque probes the continuing acute pertinence of the patterns of existence of gardens, which have not ceased to haunt the individual and collective imagination.

References
• Yves Abrioux, *Ian Hamilton Finlay: A Visual Primer* (2nd ed), Reaktion Books, London, 1992.
• Stephen Bann, 'A Description of Stonypath', *Journal of Garden History*, I, 2, 1981.
• Stephen Bann, 'From Captain Cook to Neil Armstrong: Colonial Exploration and the Structure of Landscape', in Simon Pugh (ed), *Reading Landscape: Country, City, Capital*, Manchester University Press, Manchester, 1990.
• John Barrell, *The Dark Side of the Landscape: The Rural Poor in English Painting, 1730-1840*, Cambridge University Press, Cambridge, 1980.
• Lucius Burkhardt, 'La Promenadologie', in *Le Design au-delà du visible*, Editions du Centre Pompidou, Paris, 1991.
• Burattoni & Abrioux, 'Ektopias: Two Landscapes of the Ideal', proceedings of the 4th Conference of the International Association of Word and Image Studies, Dublin, 1996, publication forthcoming.
• Ian Hamilton Finlay, 'Footnotes to an Essay', in Abrioux, *op cit*.
• Michel Foucault, 'Des éspaces autres', in *Dits et écrits* vol 4, Gallimard, Paris, 1994.
• GWF Hegel, *Journal of a Tour in the Bernese Alps*, 1796.
• John Dixon Hunt, *L'Art du jardin et son histoire*, Editions Odile Jacob, Paris, 1996.
• Bernard Lassus (ed), *Hypothèses pour une troisième nature*, Cercle Charles-Rivière Dufresny, Paris/Coracle Press, London, 1992.
• WJT Mitchell (ed), *Landscape and Power*, University of Chicago Press, 1994.
• *New Arcadians' Journal*, 1981-1997.
• Monique Mosser and Philippe Nys (eds), *Le Jardin, art et lieu de mémoire*, Les Editions de l'Imprimeur, Besançon, 1995.
• Erwin Panofsky, '*Et in Arcadia Ego*: On the Conception of Transience in Poussin and Watteau', in R Klibansky and HJ Paton (eds), *Philosophy and History: Essays Presented to Ernst Cassirer*, Oxford University Press, Oxford, 1938.
• Panofsky, '*Et in Arcadia Ego*: Poussin and the Elegiac Tradition', in *Meaning and the Visual Arts*, Doubleday Anchor, New York, 1955.
• Robert Smithson, 'A Sedimentation of Mind: Earth Projects', in Nancy Holt (ed), *The Writings of Robert Smithson*, New York University Press, New York, 1979.
• Smithson, 'Frederick Law Olmstead and the Dialectical Landscape', *ibid*.
• Frances Yates, *The Art of Memory*, Routledge and Kegan Paul, London, 1966.

MONUMENTAL MONOCHROME LANDSCAPE GENERATOR
BURATTONI & ABRIOUX

Landscapes are situated at the edge of the private and the public spheres. They are neither simply real nor purely imaginary. The term 'picturesque' clearly indicates that the gaze, which does not merely contemplate but actually composes landscapes, is impregnated with painterly codes and motifs.

Our Landscape Generator employs the logic (if not necessarily the stylistic features) of the picturesque, in order to create an installation conceived in terms of a notional garden. It fixes a chosen landscape in a monochrome state close to evanescence, while also programming possible modifications in accordance with changes in place and/or time. The Generator is designed to give individuals or institutions the chance to acquire a landscape feature – in size, the equivalent (indoors) of a domestic garden; in conception, the transposition of a much wider proprietary prospect or imaginative vision – while at the same time exposing to public view the gaze which both constructed and continues to caress their chosen vista.

The landscape will be chosen from a series of photographs taken for or by the participating individual or institution, within a precisely defined area around the place where it is to be installed. The photographs will be taken within a limited period of time. Possible subjects and aesthetic angles will be discussed with the artists. Reproductions of painted landscapes housed in the museum of the participant's own memory may also be included.

The selected landscape will be engraved by the artists on a specially prepared monochrome section of wall, in a room containing at least three windows. The chosen site will be the same size and shape as the windows.

Two of the windows will be covered with translucent veils, each of a different colour which will impregnate the monumental landscape and the air of the room in which it is sited. The third window will be left untouched.

Each individual gaze will be free to decide whether the four surfaces thus defined are to be treated as pictures, screens or openings.

In rooms lacking the required number of windows, a wall of video screens blankly emitting randomly changing monochrome coloured light may be used to colour the atmosphere.

In order to preserve the delicate balance between the public and private domains, which the Generator requires if it is to function properly, the work will exist in an edition of three.

The conditions according to which an installation may be renewed and/or displaced will be agreed with the artists at the moment of sale.

The appropriate documentation will be displayed whenever the work is exhibited in a public or commercial space.

Fifteen years after having ceded the Generator to an individual or institution, the artists will cease to exercise control over future versions of the monumental landscape.

Any individual or institution acquiring the Generator will agree to abide by the foregoing conditions and to ensure that they are adhered to if ever the Generator is sold or put out on loan.

A prototype of the *Monumental Landscape Generator* was exhibited at the Galerie Polaris, Paris, May – June 1997. The photographs were taken by Catherine Davenas, at the request of the gallery's director, Bernard Utudjian. The installation was completed by an inscription running along two walls, adapted from Sir Joshua Reynolds' *Discourses on Art*: 'LANDSCAPING, AS FAR AS LANDSCAPING IS AN ART, OR ENTITLED TO THAT APPELLATION, IS A DEVIATION FROM NATURE; FOR IF THE TRUE TASTE CONSISTS, AS MANY HOLD, IN BANISHING ANY APPEARANCE OF ART, OR ANY TRACES OF THE FOOTSTEPS OF MAN, IT WOULD THEN NO LONGER BE A LANDSCAPE.'

THE POWER OF BEAUTY
RONALD JONES

'Dislodge the Present Positions' reads one of the 400 pages that comprise Rem Koolhaas' proposal submitted for the competition to design the forthcoming expansion of the Museum of Modern Art, New York. That very theme is often heard amongst landscape designers, indeed it reverberates through books such as MOMA's own *Denatured Visions: Landscape Culture in the Twentieth Century*. But it is rarely acted upon. It seems that the profession is riddled with anxiety, as it has a difficult time finding meaningful bearings in this period after modernism. And while it is not the case that 'The art of the garden is dead', as Achille Duchene wrote in 1937, only occasional efforts have been undertaken to revive or resuscitate something, anything. Vincent Scully stated, '. . . in the modern age, and especially with that architecture we have most identified as 'modern', we have on the whole shaped the Earth badly. We need to revive our traditions and begin again.'

In his slippery essay 'Whither the Garden?' within the pages of *Denatured Visions*, Steven R Krog lays another indictment, similar to Scully's, at the foot of landscape architecture. It reads, 'With the best of intentions, landscape architecture has appropriated the images of modern art and oriental gardens but – out of ignorance, convenience, or deliberation – failed to comprehend the ideas that generated those images.' His frank and true declaration echoes forth from Christopher Tunnard's watershed *Gardens in the Modern Landscape* published in 1938. As he wrote his book the profession of landscape architecture was staggering under its own conservatism and dogged allegiance to the beaux-arts tradition of garden design. Tunnard hoped to eclipse stale convention with approaches both startling and modern by nominating three fresh design 'techniques' which included 'functionalism', the 'oriental influence', and 'modern art'. Krog accurately estimates that, 'The soul of Tunnard's book was an authentic and deeply felt 1938 crisis of belief regarding the way gardens were failing to respond to changing times.' In that spirit, the profession is presently hunting for the heir to Tunnard's vision, but at the same time is hesitant to embrace contemporary culture as a source. Oddly enough, Krog puts Jean Cocteau up to speak for him on this matter, 'To be up-to-date is to be quickly out-of-date.'

Our contemporary fretting over the way gardens are failing to respond to changing times, is part and parcel of our culture's strict artistic hierarchies and the long-standing difference between the status of the 'artist' and that of the landscape architect, or landscape designer. Remember for the moment that MOMA has only ever given one landscape architect a solo exhibition when it chose to exhibit the work of Roberto Burle Marx in a small ground floor gallery. Jasper Johns recently, and rightfully was given several floors. Ours is a culture in which the conjuror of creativity, the 'artist' is always a place occupied by the likes of Johns, Georgia O'Keefe, or Robert Smithson, but never by designers, fashion, graphic, industrial, landscape or otherwise. Where there seems to be common ground between landscape designers and artists is a territory populated by earth artists; the profession of landscape architecture is generally held in high esteem, but never by designers themselves. Richard Long, Robert Smithson, Nancy Holt, Michael Heizer, Ian Hamilton Finlay, Walter de Maria and Isamu Noguchi are among those whose work is framed by the sentiment of landscape architecture.

There has been no relief from the debilitating apprehension landscape architects feel over their status as artists, or for that matter 'architects'. It is a degree of anxiety that seems to surface in all sorts of ways, all of them uncomely. For example, witness the defensive shrill in Krog's voice when he blurts out, 'Consider the *competition* [my italics]: Julian Schnabel successfully markets paintings composed of broken dinner plates and deer antlers; Eric Fischl paints teenagers masturbating in suburban backyards; and Anselm Kiefer creates foreboding images mindful of the Holocaust.' I am not sure where the purpose of this panicky comparison with the 'competition' lies, except in highlighting, once again, the pain over status. A comparison between masturbating teens, marketing broken plates and landscape design does not take us very far in the direction criticism needs to go; all that anxiety compounds an already difficult problem. I recall that Cornel West rightfully laments the way critics and artists condemn themselves to manufacturing 'change' by consistently constructing alternatives as an escalation of radicalism rather than by inventing new forms. He would be right to deplore Krog's tail chasing.

I would rather carry the comparison in the other direction, remembering how Luis Barragan understood a garden to be first and foremost an expression of serenity, and that Terence Harkness has written with compassion and intelligence that gardens express 'enduring affection for the beauty and character of a particular place.' Is it not true that the art of landscape design is creating myth, style, history, memory, but most of all beauty? And yet landscape designers and critics often long for this work to mean something more – something more seriously artistic: Why? Endlessly self-conscious about their relationship to high culture through beauty, critics and designers often seem self-deprecating about the way beauty lends merit to landscape design.

I believe that, in a fundamental way, the practice of landscape architecture aspires to a special appreciation of beauty aligned with Dave Hickey's nomination of beauty as an overwhelming and powerful tool. Hickey has written:

> The task of these figures of beauty was to enfranchise the audience and acknowledge its power – to designate a territory of shared values between the image and its beholder and, then, in this territory, to argue the argument by valorising the picture's problematic content.

Hickey is right, and he has splendidly applied this argument to the photographs of Robert Mapplethorpe. In its most compelling moments the landscape designed creates shared values within the culture of the beautiful, and having done that confronts difficult or unsettled content. Maya Lin comes easily to mind, as well as Bomarzo's explicit opposition to the nominal vision of utopia. Hickey's words underline my point about landscape architecture: designers need not aspire to a kind of artistic power their work already possesses, and in measures that make it abundantly clear how the very same content hovers somewhere near zero in much contemporary fine art, and museum culture. Is this what Krog was trying to say through his tantrum?

Of course the weight of the hand of landscape design can be felt on history's larger swells. There have been moments in history when landscape designers actually participated directly in the evolution of their culture, moments in which the call went forth for fundamental change, and the public responded. I think of the obvious examples, like Haussmann's green metropolis. But contemplate for a moment the continuing struggle over the humble domain of People's Park, New York, or the decision by Albert Speer to link the Viktoriapark in Berlin to the Tempelhof Airport along a great architectural axis that would bond an abiding Teutonic religion of wood spirits, of *Blut und Boden*, with the future of the absolute tyranny of modern power. Why weren't Matisse, Ben Shawn, or Picasso this enterprising? As artists, they were never positioned to be the agency for change, to argue the argument, to valorise problematic content through Hickey's appreciation of beauty. They were capable of picturing the prospect of reform, or change – but never the instrument, or site for its creation.

In a recent interview the illustrator Matt Mahurin said, 'The painting of a war scene can be as powerful as any photograph of a war scene.' I am certain he is wrong, and why? Mahurin is blind and uncritical in the way he, like landscape designers, privileges the position of the artist. Art possesses no internal guidance system that gives it the power to do more than be a looking glass, often with astounding capabilities at magnifying an artist's self-interest, or, offering a perspective on our culture. It is rare that art does more than point at its subject. Condemned to the status of a refracting device, its only option is to create its voice out of the second person. That is not surprising nor condemning, but only a serviceable description of what much art may aspire to do.

Robert Smithson's film about the *Spiral Jetty* makes self-evident that – as with playwrights, and I would add here landscape designers – artistic success depends on how completely exterior conditions fade from view. Walking out onto the jetty is not the experience of the unwinding path indelibly etched onto our minds by the familiar aerial photographs, but a long low and immanently thin horizontal view of rocks and earth at your feet. Turning towards the centre and making one's way along the path, one is finally left with oneself. Objectivity, which produced the spiral from above, fades during the trip; it is lost at ground level as the nominal subject–object relationship collapses. Such an experience is strongly related to the disappearance of the signified into the sign that unfolds with the encounter of Buttes-Chaumont, Paris, Central Park, New York or Finlay's Stonypath. Experience shifts from the second to the first person; and this shift is central to landscape architecture's greatest artistic assets. Such experiences become radical, and original precisely because their resistance to conventional experiences of art seems so passive. They have, as Cornel West wishes, bypassed the escalation of radicality and invented new forms. And that, I believe, is one of the most important reasons artists so often aspire to the power and beauty of landscape design.

CAESAR'S COSMIC GARDEN

RONALD JONES

Of all the aerial photographs taken of Auschwitz-Birkenau during the final year of the Second World War, one stands out above all the others. The photograph I have in mind was taken on 25 August, 1944, and was obviously intended to document the Gas Chamber and Crematorium II in the southwest corner of the camp. Like the others, this picture bore labels applied by Allied photo interpreters that identified buildings and various incriminating sites. Mostly they were labels one would expect to find on this sort of picture: 'gas chamber', 'undressing room', and 'possible cremation pit'. But one label was unexpected. Gazing down into the picture it is clear to see that within a few yards of the crematorium there was a formal garden whose design is easily recognisable as the cosmic plan. The photo interpreters did not decipher its plan, but chose to label the garden descriptively, 'landscape'. Traditionally, the centre of a cosmic plan represents the Earth and is created out of four intersecting paths which represent the rivers of paradise. Typically a tree or fountain will appear at the garden's centre. The designers of the garden for Crematorium II chose to feature a tree. Because the garden was situated between the 'entrance gate' and the 'undressing room', one has to imagine that for hundreds of thousands the unexpected garden provided their final glimpse of the world.

Certainly the garden was planted and maintained by the *Abteilung Landwirtschaft* or The Agricultural Division stationed at Auschwitz. Under the direction of Dr Joachim Caesar this had become an important enterprise within the camp as early as 1941. Himmler, who had been an agriculturist, looked favourably upon Caesar's creation of the *Landwirtschaftskommando* which was made up of prisoners assigned to cultivate the camp's landscape. One of their most important duties was to plant tall hedges around many of the gas chambers and crematoria. The hedges or *Grüngürtel* (greenbelt) were put up to disguise the inevitable from the uninitiated. Plainly said, camp administrators feared that the awful reality masked by the hedge would unnecessarily alarm those being marched to the showers. The cosmic garden was planted after the hedge went in around Gas Chamber and Crematoria II, and therefore the timing invites the conclusion that the garden was originally, and only, intended for the eyes of those about to be gassed. Who decided to plant this garden, creating this small intersection of paradise within the belly of evil?

This poignant question has never been far from my mind since I first saw the aerial photographs as a child. And it was only recently answered within a passage from Harold Bloom's book *The Anxiety of Influence*. Bloom, not at all thinking of the Holocaust, compares the aspiration of Milton's Satan with a poet's artistic desire by imagining his fall from Grace and stinging arrival in Hell. Bloom reports that there was no flinching when Satan faced up to his circumstances. He was, by Bloom's account a dignified realist, 'either repent and surrender your selfhood,' Satan reasoned, 'or create a relative goodness out of radical evil.' The rest of that story is history.

Who was the dignified realist who authored the garden behind the hedge at Gas Chamber and Crematoria II? It was certainly a member of the *Landwirtschaftskommando*. Typically those assigned to the *Landwirtschaftskommando* were not immediately marked for death but were often like Anna Urbanova, a German Catholic who was condemned to Auschwitz as a political dissident. Unlike most of those who arrived at Auschwitz, Anna possessed an option exceedingly rare within concentration camps. It was the same option thrust upon Milton's Satan. Anna and the others who built the cosmic plan garden could 'repent', relinquishing their selfhood in order to join with their oppressors, or sustain their selfhood by exploring the limits of damnation, hoping to find a relative goodness. The garden traces the limits of damnation and resonates with salvation only available near the heart of radical evil.

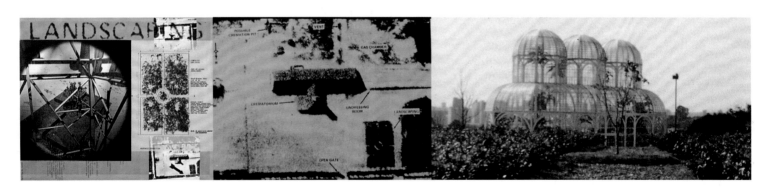

PFLANZENZUCHT TANGO
RONALD JONES

The title *pflanzenzucht tango*, is derived from the German phrase meaning plant cultivation and was the name for the division of inmates that attended to landscaping at Auschwitz-Birkenau. Three bonsai gardens were included in the installation, and were titled: *The Fall*, *Paradise* and *Wilderness*. The first two bonsai gardens reproduced designs of gardens representing hell and heaven, and the third was a reproduction of the Auschwitz-Birkenau prisoners' cosmic garden plan. The plan for *The Fall*, was quoted from the 1618 engraving *The Rationalisation of the Fall*, and the plan for *Paradise* came from the 1617 engraving *Animals Before the Entrance to the Garden of Eden*. Completing the elements of the installation are: a scrim painting of a 1635 garden scene depicting a man seducing a woman while Death looks on. The man observes the figure of Death through a reversed telescope making the haunting figure appear to be farther away than it is. An antique telescope reversed and mounted atop a ladder pierces the scrim from behind and is aimed at the bonsai garden *The Fall*. Three tango soundscapes, one composed for each garden by Todd Levin are included as audio components of the installation. Three computer-generated cactus prints depicting each of the gardens completes the installation.

OPPOSITE FROM L TO R: The Kommando Pflanzenzucht's Cosmic Garden, *1995, 101.6x127 cm; aerial photo of Auschwitz-Birkenau,* Caesar's Cosmic Garden, *1995, Fundacao Cultural de Curitiba, Brazil; view of* Caesar's Cosmic Garden, *1995, Fundacao Cultural de Curitiba, Brazil; FROM ABOVE:* Wilderness, *1993-95, 166.37x53.34x38.1 cm;* The Fall, *1995, from I David's 'paradisus sponsi et Spon Sae', 1618, 109.2x57.15x55.88cm;* Paradise, *1995, 166.37x53.34x38.1 cm;* Wilderness, *detail, each bonsai garden on wooden base; installation Metro Pictures, New York*

PLANTS AND DESIGN

CHARLES CHESSHIRE

When we look out over a 17th-century European garden of grass, topiary, hedges and trees it may be easy to forget the presence of living plants and the workings of time upon them. In these gardens plants such as box, yew, hornbeam or beech have become so abstracted from their natural form that they have become walls, doors and floors. If you were to walk over Box Hill in Surrey you couldn't help but admire the fantastic wild shape of the old box trees and then perhaps find it hard to reconcile the tortured status that it has found as a hedge. In parts of New England you can see where old box hedges that border paths have been neglected retrieving some of their natural habit, and where the new owners have clearly decided to keep their new shape. This too has happened to the pillars of yew on the terraces of Powys Castle, near Welshpool, where these original architectural sentinels now resemble immense green clouds rolling over the walls. The degree to which a plant will allow itself to be abstracted until it has lost its original identity and the degree of a plant's powerful individual presence will determine its status in garden design. Some plants are so overtly ornamental in their every part that to place them in a garden would give them status as an *objet d'art*, unless perhaps when they are planted *en masse*, whereas others can modestly yield to being part of the artist's media.

Before European plant collectors started scouring the globe for everything and anything, gardens to a large degree had retained a simplicity, whether it was the great gardens of Le Nôtre or even the gardens of Japan. For example, by the end of the 19th century there were perhaps only 50 or so species of rhododendron known in England, mostly from the USA. Twenty years later this had gone up to 200, almost all of them from China (with hybrids this has risen to thousands today). China's flora turned out to be an immense untapped reservoir, yet to the Chinese these plants were worthless and usually nameless. They had no role to play in their gardens. The Chinese gardens grew pines, bamboo, lotus, chrysanthemums, tree peonies, mulberries, as well as a few others for their medicinal or symbolic virtues. This limited repertoire was inherited by the Japanese who added azaleas, cherries and maples. But even to the Japanese the azalea was often not there as the glorious extrovert that we know in the West but as a plant that could be manipulated into shapes to evoke elements of the landscape outside the garden like hills and forests. Indeed the azaleas are often clipped to the point that they are no longer able to flower. The azalea in Japan has perhaps the same potentially abstract status that the box has in Europe. Pines are also deliberately contorted and plucked to evoke old age and the idealised forms of the wild pines of Japan's windswept coasts and islands. They have become part of the oriental picturesque, where gardens are often copies of ancient landscape paintings.

The principle of a restricted plant vocabulary enables the garden designer to abstract more easily. The more diverse the planting, the more the plants are allowed to be simply themselves, the more figurative the 'picture' becomes. All the great gardens of the world such as Versailles, the Katsura palace in Kyoto, the Renaissance gardens of Italy or the later landscape gardens of England all relied on simplicity in their language of plants. The latter was later to evolve into the Picturesque movement with painting, poetry and philosophy as its sources of inspiration. In these gardens, plants had merged to become one with the design. In a sense the English had reached a kind of pinnacle in artistry with this style of design, this oneness. One of the earliest examples of the landscape garden was Stourhead in Wiltshire (*c*1730) with its wooded hillsides around an elegant lake punctuated by follies. By the late 19th century, these woods had been filled with exotics, rhododendrons in particular, to the point that in May and June they have become a spectacle that totally detracts from the original design. Purists will only visit this garden outside the rhododendron season while thousands of others will visit in order to see the colour. The plant as individual has the power to overwhelm and seduce the viewer away from the intended experience of the sublime. In the one extreme the plant is manipulated into complete submission to design and in the other it has the complete ability to overwhelm it.

In England all the poetry of the Picturesque was lost at the dawn of the Industrial Revolution. Hot houses and tropical exotics, as well as a less enlightened elite, revealed an irresistible urge to display the plants as trophies. In the 18th century, the trophy had been the style, power and politics that could be bought or collected in the form of designers such as William Kent, Capability Brown or Humphrey Repton but by the mid-1800s it was the turn of the plants and man's overt cleverness at their cultivation.

By the end of the 19th century a new revolution was taking place, fronted by William Robinson with the encouragement of Gertrude Jekyll, and this was a plea to return to a wilder form of gardening and to the handling of plants with the care and

FROM ABOVE, L TO R: Palazzo Piccolomini, terrace, 1460, Pienza; André Le Nôtre, the garden of Vaux-le-Vicomte, 1658; Villa Lante, Bagnaia, groto, 1566; Rousham, box hedge, c1738, Oxfordshire

FROM L TO R: Caerhays Castle, early 1900s, Cornwall; The White Garden, Sissinghurst, 1930s

sensitivity that was symbolised by the old cottage gardener. It was a romantic movement but one that was truly serious and that railed against the Victorian carpet bedding (this can be seen today in William Nesfield's restored garden in Regent's Park). Now, a century later, this revolution seems to have returned again but this time as a reaction to lost nature and wilderness.

Robinson's crusade for wild gardening found some unlikely allies in the early 1900s in the planters of the new discoveries from the Orient. These wealthy landowners and sponsors of the great plant collectors planted their gardens with great care. They responded to every detail the collector gave them and then sought the closest conditions in their gardens which would suit them. The result was, in places like Caerhays Castle in Cornwall and Bodnant in North Wales, gardens that also achieved a kind of unity but one based on chance and science even though the results were often quite artful, and very close to a kind of Eden. These gardens in turn also became perverted and cluttered by the more garish cultivars that followed and by plants from mixed provenances, and as at Stourhead have become adventures in pure spectacle.

It is hard for any garden artist or designer to resist the charms of plants, to exercise restraint in their use, but all the successful gardeners have had to. Burle Marx warned against creating a fruit salad out of mixed plantings. Except in a few cases the style of the English garden has become downgraded to a craft of cultivating plants in different and usually indifferent compositions. Gertrude Jekyll wrote on her observations of the wildwoods of southern England in her book *Wood and Garden* (1899) that, 'no artificial planting can ever equal that of Nature, but one may learn from it the great lesson of the importance of moderation and reserve, of simplicity of intention, and directness of purpose, and the inestimable value of the quality called "breadth" in painting.' This gentility and reserve has come to personify the ideal of the English garden. Here the plants are all, bouquets of them, bringing elegance, perfume, memories and complete pleasure. The garden had become the place of skilled craft, and the designer's hand become disguised beneath airs of deliberate sophistication.

After two world wars – with the combination of austerities on the one hand and the advent of the age of convenience and the disposable on the other – plants had a new role to play. They had to fit an new ideal, to be evergreen, self-maintaining, groundcovering and possess 'all year round interest'. This was a period of Pop art for plants which brought in a host of plants like dwarf conifers, heathers, hypericums and cotoneasters which today are the fodder of the municipal landscaper. Gardens of this period are instantly identifiable by the plants in them but are already fading into obscurity except in public parks and supermarket car-parks.

Of the plants that are in favour today, one of the most successful has been grass. Grasses, not being overtly ornamental but being 'inert' enough that they lend themselves to mass planting and yet play an intermediary role between the lawn and the wilderness, have found themselves being used to great effect in Europe and the USA, in both ultra formal designs, such as those by Jacques Wirtz or earlier in a more playful way by Russell Page. The old reliable yew and box have returned and many of the species of plants, whose hybrids had previously superseded them, have returned to

FROM L TO R: Russell Page, Grass Borders, 1980, Pepsico Headquarters, Purchase, New York; Alain Pellissier (architect) and Fujiko Nakaya (designer), Mist Garden, 1986, Parc de la Villette, Paris

display an airier sophistication and a closer commune to nature. Needless to say in a period when fashions fade with each glossy magazine, such trends are peppered by weeks when big, bold and brassy is in or the next it might be architectural plants, or perhaps the jungle or meadows. Today, though, both public and designers are becoming remarkably and increasingly well informed about plants and are becoming very specific in their choices, often going to great lengths to find them through publications such as *The Plant Finder* which now lists over 60,000 varieties.

At the turn of yet another century several pictures are emerging. One is the ultra contemporary view of a modern high-tech world where sophisticated artist-designers substitute plants altogether with imitations in plastic or metal, particularly in Japan, and where the blurred lines of sculpture, installations and gardens meet but where the artist is master. Charles Jencks has managed to create meaning with only grass and trees, similar in some respects to 18th-century landscape gardens, while Ian Hamilton Finlay has also to some extent relied on the *genius loci*.

In the experimental gardens at Chaumont-sur-Loire it is possible to see the extremes to which plants will bow to the constraints of the designer. Some plants look distinctly uncomfortable when asked to perform tricks. Nature and natural form are too strong to be torn away too far from their roots. More sympathetic are the formulaic ecological plantings being promoted in Germany and Holland which, although working in sympathy with the plant's needs, show no evidence of any positive design direction except as an expression of environmental awareness. The results of some of the latter evoke some of the principles of William Robinson and of great gardens like Caerhays but, for a serious designer, it is more of a horticultural system than a real artistic principle.

Gilles Clément is perhaps one of the most successful of plantsman-designers today and in his garden in the centre of Blois he pays homage to his own French tradition where the characteristics of Le Nôtre are still clearly there, but his planting shows a wonderful break. In particular his parterres of undulating yew hedges contain between them a mixture of plants more often associated with wild gardens or deep 'mixed borders'. But these giant perennials seem quite happy contained in narrow parterres because Clément has mastered their association. The overall effect is of a modern garden that is both formal and yet celebrates the individual beauty of plants, while the plants themselves have had all their 'design potential' harnessed to a maximum. Clément equally achieved this in his Silver Garden in the Parc André Citroën, where his style is distinctly Japanese, the plants placed in a similar way to the rocks at the Ryoanji in Kyoto, but again the plants are not tortured or abstracted but fully harnessed to evoke the flow of a river.

The plant's greatest ally is time, where the designer often has to wait in the fourth dimension for his vision to complete. Often the plants will surpass him and add their version of artistry beyond his intention, or even consume his original design altogether. Plants as artists' material appear on the one hand immensely flexible, while on the other they have too much charm to be insulted or too much character to be manipulated.

(photos Charles Chesshire)

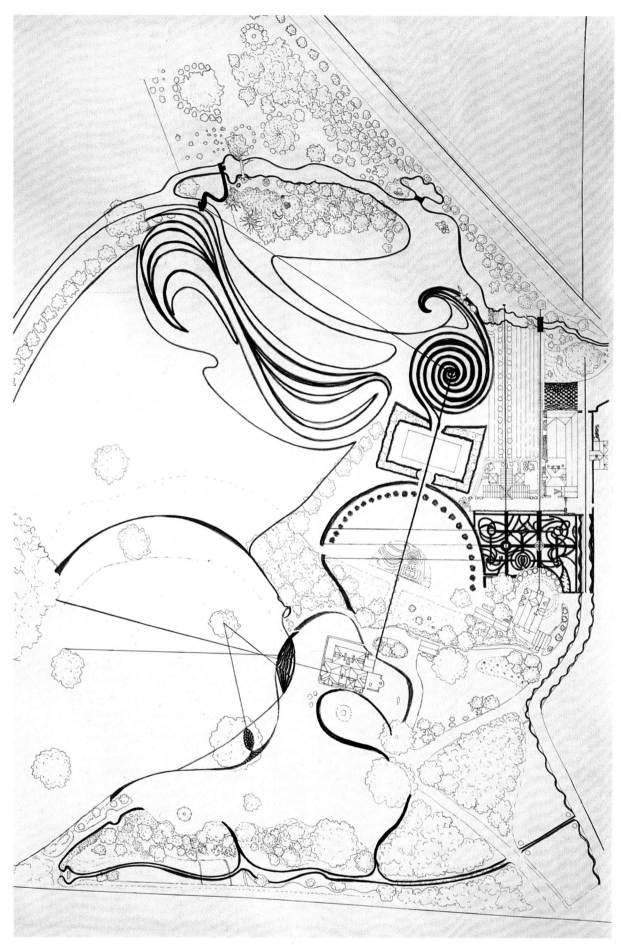

Figure 3. *Plan of garden, drawn with Madelon Vriesendorp. Visible here are, middle right to left: Common Sense Garden (Physics and DNA); Sense of Fair Play (tennis court); Sense of Twist. Below centre are visible the Symmetry Break Terrace, Black Hole and other twists.*

THE UNIVERSE AS MEASURE

CHARLES JENCKS

Why focus on the universe as a subject for architecture or landscape? The answer has a compelling logic. First, all art forms necessarily have an iconography, style and subject matter – even abstract ones – so why not focus on the most significant entity, the one from which we originate? Second, a negative reason: religions and the belief in historical metanarratives, such as progress, are in decline, and there is no unifying narrative adequate to the emergent global culture except the story of the universe, its historical unfolding. Third, the universe is prior to the earth and humanity – it is primary – and, lastly, we naturally identify with, or want to relate to, the cosmos. When a friend dies, we take our grief to nature.

There are many emotional reasons, if these are allowed as rational, for focusing on the cosmos, but here I will mention public, interpersonal ones since architecture and landscape are public languages. The universe is not only the biggest and oldest thing around but, epistemologically speaking, the most generative. It is the grounding for everything, the final foundation or, in Renaissance language, the measure of all things.

This may be granted but, as Woody Allen complained, 'What has the universe ever done for me?' It seems indifferent to our fate and, what's worse, occasionally vicious. Furthermore, Darwinian nature is supposedly 'red in tooth and claw' and even inanimate nature is violent when supernovae blow up. Its terror and destruction are real – the universe alienates as well as inspires – but it has one overwhelming virtue: it gives birth to everything, it is highly creative, sustaining, interesting and, on occasion, beautiful. What else is there? Other universes, perhaps, but we'll never know for certain.

I want to sketch an active strategy for art, architecture and culture in general. If the universe is the grounding for action and value, it becomes the referent for culture, but not a passive one. The universe, as we perceive it, is partly coloured by our theories and preconceptions and partly changed through reinterpretation with new metaphors and understandings. It may have its vicious moments, but we owe it the respect and love we show a parent – albeit a complex one. This attitude of ironic love and profound respect is a developed taste, a frame of mind found in several scientists and cosmologists who make the study of the universe their passion. In a way, one could say it is a religious or spiritual attitude, except these words have become too tired and imprecise. A new language, both verbal and visual, is needed to get us back into a palpable relationship with the universe. Hence, for me, 'the garden of cosmic speculation', a garden in Scotland which my late wife, Maggie Keswick, and I started work on in 1990.

Cosmic speculation? Speculating means accepting the facts and interpretations of how things are, and then going beyond them. It means confronting the way the universe unfolds, its physical laws, its basic principles of development, its direction and, above all, its history. All of these points have come into sharp focus in the last 20 years. We can tell the story of the universe, from the first few seconds, as a continuous narrative of development – as a drama of increasing complexity – and we can give many of the reasons for its unfolding. Narrative and complexity theory, story and explanation, these are two sides of an arch which are coming together with great strength. While not every part is complete, the structure stands up to scrutiny and works.

Phase transitions – Jumps

The first point to make about the cosmos is that it is a process and not a static entity; it is 'cosmogenic' not 'cosmic'. Furthermore, we know something that previous ages did not: as well as evolving gradually, it tends to shift suddenly from one phase to another, to self-organise continuously at different levels, a process I have characterised as 'jumping'.

The four major phase transitions since the origin of the universe have been from energy to matter to life to consciousness. These four jumps, and countless lesser ones which happen at different scales, comprise its history (figure 1). Nature's way of evolving, as Stephen Jay Gould and others show, is to undergo sudden punctuations – not just the continuous, gradual developments predicated by Darwin. So, living nature and inanimate matter both evolve through shifts, leaps, catastrophes – as well as continuous variation.

How can the designer present the dynamism of this story? Speculation means constant questioning, seeing that the presentation of nature's laws are not entirely determined, but open to partial reinterpretation. One can reject the metaphor of the Standard Model, such as the 'Big Bang', and question the orthodoxy (nearly every scientist uses this and its counterpart for The End, the 'Big Crunch', or another outcome, 'The Heat Death'). Ninety-five percent of the universe is said to be dark matter – termed 'WIMPS' or 'MACHOS'. No wonder people are alienated from nature, with metaphors like these: but they can be questioned. The origin of the universe was not 'big', but smaller than a quark; it was not a 'bang', no one heard it; it was

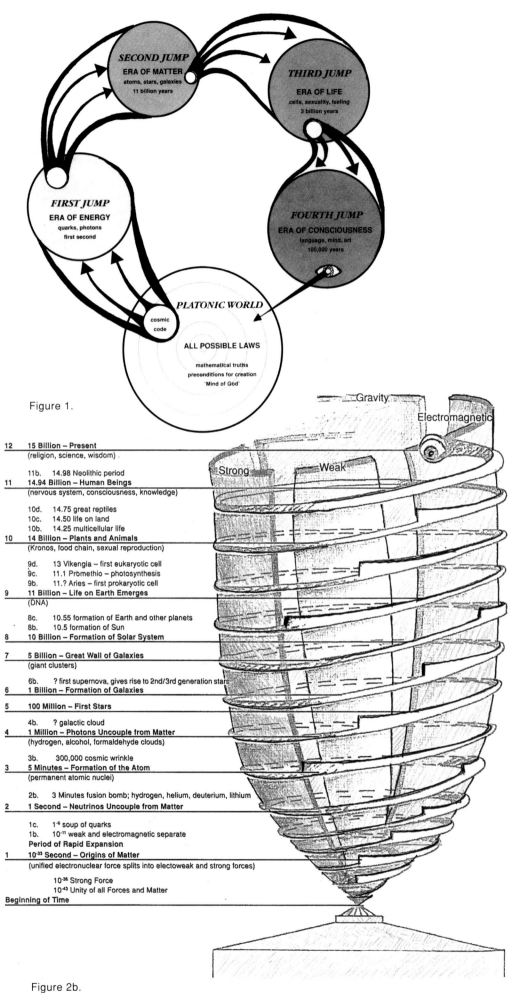

Figure 1.

Figure 1 diagram labels

SECOND JUMP
ERA OF MATTER
atoms, stars, galaxies
11 billion years

THIRD JUMP
ERA OF LIFE
cells, sexuality, feeling
3 billion years

FIRST JUMP
ERA OF ENERGY
quarks, photons
first second

FOURTH JUMP
ERA OF CONSCIOUSNESS
language, mind, art
100,000 years

PLATONIC WORLD

cosmic code

ALL POSSIBLE LAWS

mathematical truths
preconditions for creation
'Mind of God'

Figure 2a.

Figure 2b timeline

Gravity

Electromagnetic

Strong Weak

12	15 Billion – Present
	(religion, science, wisdom)
11b.	14.98 Neolithic period
11	14.94 Billion – Human Beings
	(nervous system, consciousness, knowledge)
10d.	14.75 great reptiles
10c.	14.50 life on land
10b.	14.25 multicellular life
10	14 Billion – Plants and Animals
	(Kronos, food chain, sexual reproduction)
9d.	13 Vikengia – first eukaryotic cell
9c.	11.1 Promethio – photosynthesis
9b.	11.? Aries – first prokaryotic cell
9	11 Billion – Life on Earth Emerges
	(DNA)
8c.	10.55 formation of Earth and other planets
8b.	10.5 formation of Sun
8	10 Billion – Formation of Solar System
7	5 Billion – Great Wall of Galaxies
	(giant clusters)
6b.	? first supernova, gives rise to 2nd/3rd generation stars
6	1 Billion – Formation of Galaxies
5	100 Million – First Stars
4b.	? galactic cloud
4	1 Million – Photons Uncouple from Matter
	(hydrogen, alcohol, formaldehyde clouds)
3b.	300,000 cosmic wrinkle
3	5 Minutes – Formation of the Atom
	(permanent atomic nuclei)
2b.	3 Minutes fusion bomb; hydrogen, helium, deuterium, lithium
2	1 Second – Neutrinos Uncouple from Matter
1c.	1^{-6} soup of quarks
1b.	10^{-11} weak and electromagnetic separate
	Period of Rapid Expansion
1	10^{-33} Second – Origins of Matter
	(unified electronuclear force splits into electoweak and strong forces)
	10^{-36} Strong Force
	10^{-43} Unity of all Forces and Matter
	Beginning of Time

Figure 2b.

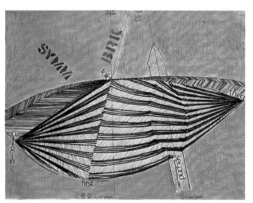

Figure 2c.

not like the explosion of a firecracker, but actually the inflation of space. In fact, because it was the stretching of space between plasma and matter, it should really be called the 'Hot Stretch'. A scientist who gives it a moment of thought would agree. In a similar dialectic, all metaphors which ground us to the universe are partially open to rethinking – constrained by the evidence, but not fixed. We make the choice of our metaphors, and then they choose our future. It is the architect and designer's role to get them right – or at least better than others.

In one model I have conceived the universe as a holistic globe spiralling out from a centre, like a wave gathering momentum (figure 2a). In another, based on the same evidence, it is presented as an expanding trumpet, with 30 leaps marked as steps (figure 2b). The same narrative can be portrayed in yet a third metaphor: in a garden terrace the four jumps are dramatised as symmetry breaks in a pattern of grass and pebbles (figure 2c). These end in the leap of consciousness: a growing hedge that will fly over the wall and terrace. Thus there are three different solutions, all compatible with the standard model of the universe and all alternatives to the metaphor of the Big Bang. They show that from the same scientific theories different interpretations can be drawn – and this difference is a freedom for the architect. They also show that where scientists often produce alienating metaphors lies a fertile territory waiting to be invented.

What are Nature's Basic Forms?

I have never understood why architects, painters and philosophers – following Plato – have thought that the ultimate reality behind things lies in straight lines, right angles and perfect, geometric solids. Nature is basically curved, warped, undulating, jagged, zig-zagged and sometimes beautifully crinkly. It never looks like a Platonic temple or a railroad track. So deep are preconceptions of God as Geometer, however, that even Western artists who spend their time painting outdoors – as did Cézanne – are apt to see the world as a proposition from Euclid's textbook. After a lifetime spent observing the landscape of Provence he insisted that 'tout est spheres et cylindres'. His painting, like that of the Cubists, may have been better for this, but the mountains and pine trees of Aix-en-Provence are not the regular geometric solids this suggests. So, are there fundamental forms behind the appearances of nature? And, if so, what are they?

One answer was recognised by the Chinese. Maggie, in researching a book on Chinese gardens, had found an apt metaphor for the Scottish landscape in which we were designing, for the soft valleys and low curving hills. Chinese landscape painters, following Taoist monks and philosophers, saw hills and mountains as 'the bones of the earth' energised with *chi*, the 'vital breath' of subterranean dragons. These metaphors became one strategy for a set of five gardens. They are pulled together by large-scale forms – giant worms or snakes – or, if one prefers the non-metaphorical, abstract

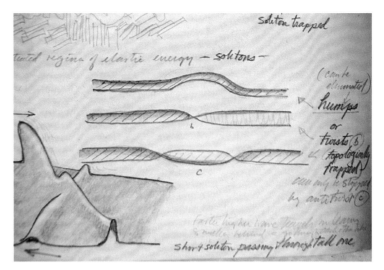

Figure 4. *Soliton Drawings, sketches from science showing trapped solitons, and energy waves going through each other – keeping a memory, not dissipating.*

Figure 5. *Soliton Wave Gates, fractal print.*

Figure 1. *Four Jumps to Consciousness. Each of the four areas emerges from the one below and is not reducible to it. Hence the different laws and realms which are, to a degree, autonomous.*

Figure 2. *Three metaphors of the universe all based on the Standard Model of science:* Figure 2a. *The Global Model, showing holistic, spherical expansion from a centre;* Figure 2b. *The Trumpet Model, or flower of steps which signify the 12 'main' jumps or 22 'minor' ones.* Figure 2c. *The Jumping Streams, four jumps, from left to right, energy, matter, life, consciousness. Symmetry Break Terrace drawings. Energy emerges in straight lines, from the left, then matter bends space and time in curved lines. The jump into life is portrayed as a concave sheer in pattern, that jumps into consciousness by the hedge that leaps over the ha-ha.*

23

twisting lines that fold over each other (figure 3).

The point is that nature's basic forms are continuously changing: self-similar not self-same. I sought a new grammar which would draw together all the elements – the hills, streams, hedges, terraces and walls. Representing a dynamic process is difficult for static architecture, as the Futurists found with their monuments to frozen movement. Yet the growing, incremental forms that Benoit Mandelbrot has explained, in *The Fractal Geometry of Nature*, reveal a suggestive approach. As he insists at the beginning of his manifesto, 'Clouds are not spheres, mountains are not cones, coastlines are not circles, and bark is not smooth, nor does lightning travel in a straight line.' Rather, most of nature is irregular, fragmented, broken – or related to his neologism coming from the Latin *fractus*. Nature does not, except in the very rare instances of planets or stars, adopt a Euclidean form. And yet, as Mandelbrot has argued, Western metaphysicians and architects have disdained non-Euclidean forms as 'amorphous' and 'pathological'.

Today the more subtle order hidden within these seeming monsters has been revealed – through the sciences of complexity. Nature's basic forms may be non-Euclidean, but that does not make them unordered. What are called 'strange attractors' or 'chaotic attractors' (the self-similar organisation emerging within chaos) underlie trees, mountain ranges as much as they do the human brain and heart. Because they are the basic forms behind nature, strange attractors became a major pattern for the design shown here. Modern and classical architecture is, by contrast, based on the repetition of the same, static pattern. The new sciences lead away from Cézanne and Le Corbusier's spheres, cones and cylinders towards new shapes of self-organisation. Self-similarity is the exemplar, not self-sameness.

Solitons

One of the many sciences of complexity concerns the theory of soliton waves, the coherent pulses of energy which underlie such things as tidal waves, nerve fibres and superconductors. Solitons were first discovered by a Scottish engineer in 1834 as he was riding horseback along the Union Canal near Edinburgh – thus providing me with a local pretext for representing the extraordinary properties of these waves. Solitons can travel through each other and still remember their past – they may also form an aspect of our memory.

In the garden they are represented in many different forms, particularly in a group of ten gates (figures 4,5,6). Here waves of energy are shown travelling through the metal elements as a series of twists. When viewed straight on these twists are seen, paradoxically, as an absence of metal – a void – and, from the side, as a travelling hump rather like the curl in a whiplash. Alternating bands of solid and void, black and white, green and gravel are repeated throughout the garden. The visual illusions provoke different readings.

Functionally, the void or hump leads the eye one way to the hinges, the other way to the latch. These key points are often picked out with fossils and a surrounding Mobius Strip, yet another twist which has interesting properties. There are also certain affinities between the curves, even that of the spiral fossils. The motivations are mixed: the metal strips must be close enough together to keep out the rabbits and far enough apart to give the optical vibrations of figure versus ground. The twists and fossils must represent coherent energy – solitons – and yet indicate mundane things: where the latch is.

A Landscape of Waves

The same mixture of practicality and aesthetic preconception is evident in the much larger waves of the landscape – a spiral mound about 50 feet high, and a series of twisting snakes 400 feet long (figures 7,8). Maggie had dug out an old marsh, creating a series of connected, curving ponds and a left-over pile of earth. We moved the pile with diggers and bulldozers and we could see that this equipment naturally generated blob-curves that were like the shape-grammar of rooms I had been designing. The scale, equipment and material – sand and gravel – make a broad-brush approach inevitable: it is hard to get earth to within four feet of the place you want it and have it stay there and accept grass. The constant rains of Western Scotland smear out all but the largest gesture, making design extremely primitive. Nevertheless, the basic ideas of twists, folds and waves of energy are in the mounds.

The snake mound first twists towards the main pond and then, in a series of terraces which warp like a race-track into the curve, they twist the other way to another garden and view. There is a certain energy and movement in these lines and in the paisley-shapes of the ponds. The snail mound is built from two different spirals (one from the head, the other from the tail) which only meet at the top, and they have the paradoxical aspect of rising and falling as they ascend. As a result, in places, in order to go up you have to go down and to go down you have to go up. It is meant to be frustrating and make you think about the difficulty of moving towards a goal. The mounds present more than a snake and snail, but these metaphors became inevitable to describe them for construction. They carry one into the larger landscape and provide a journey of continuous vertigo, like driving a racing car through a spaghetti junction of green velvet.

Wilderness of Science

Mixed metaphors are inevitable. A more formal Physics Garden, with models of the atom, Gaia, the universe and several other cosmogenic elements is in progress (figures 9,10). These were designed with scientists, metalworkers and others, but they interpret the truths of the universe through displaced and combinatorial models. They are not illustrations of contemporary science but reimaginations of what this public discourse tells

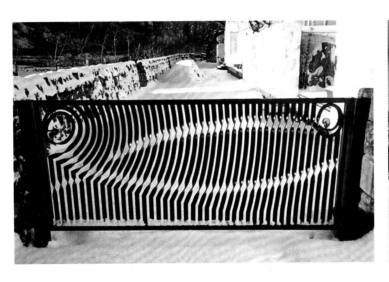

Figure 6. *Twists run through the Soliton Gates towards the latch and hinges; light and dark bands throughout the garden set up vibrating patterns and visual illusions. Wave-forms of energy, alternating waves, waves of light – photons – interfere creating overlapping waves.*

Figure 8. *Snail Mound above Snake Mound, aerial perspective. The interlacing of two spirals, which lean at an angle, force one to go both up and down when ascending (or descending).*

Figure 7. *Snake Mound orients three paths to the lake and then twists them the other way to the cattle field.*

27

us. It is important to stress the difference. We are soon bored of illustration, even that of new discoveries – such as the beautiful photographs from the Hubble telescope. Fractal patterns, or diagrams from science, both exercise the mind and eye for only a short time, until we know them completely.

So knowledge cuts two ways. We are pulled by new knowledge; it is captivating, titillating, alluring, sexy, even a drive of sentient creatures to adapt to the world. Also we are pushed by the information revolution and the emergent knowledge industries: not to know the next step in science or industry or, sometimes, art is to fall behind. But understanding the meaning of a scientific idea exhausts the drive. Aesthetic fatigue sets in after we have consummated the chase, so an art using the drive for knowledge – curiosity – also has to rely on something more. This more is imaginative translation, the turning of illustrations into a surprising language of design.

The outer language of the universe, which is slowly being decoded by scientists and others, has to be reformulated in terms of the inner languages of art and design. Ruskin and Kandinsky insisted on this double necessity. Today, in an age dominated by anthropocentrism, science presents the wilderness, an otherness, a mystery beyond politics, the economy and the consciousness industry. This remains a non-human standard and a possible public language, the truths of the universe, the universals. The question was posed by Kandinsky – can we develop the inner languages which adequately reflect these transcendent realities?

Poetics

The complex relations between artist and medium vary for each art form and its malleability. In poetry and novels we expect the written material will be transformed by the writer and anything that does not pass through this process is considered shopworn or cliched. This idea was expressed countless times in the 19th century by, among others, an obscure Russian literary critic who had a great influence on Turgenev and Tolstoy. Isaiah Berlin, in an essay 'Artistic Commitment', finds a canonic formulation by Vissarion Belinsky, which could almost be Coleridge writing on the necessary transformative powers of the imagination:

Belinsky's position is crystal clear: 'No Matter how beautiful the ideas in a poem, how powerfully it echoes the problems of the hour, if it lacks poetry, there can be no beautiful thought in it, and no problems either, and all that one may say about it is that it is a fine intention badly executed'. This is because the artist's commitment 'must be not only in the head, but above all in the heart, in the blood of the writer . . . An idea . . . which has not passed through one's own nature, has not received the stamp of one's personality, is dead capital not only for poetry, but for any literary activity.'[1]

In effect, this is a plea for the irreducible necessity of artistic emotion and willpower, the personal stamp which marks all great creations even, paradoxically, impersonal ones (where they express an artistic vision). An individual's style is like a psychic fingerprint: it covers everything the artist touches with an unmistakable identity and a way of looking at things. This orientation, this sensibility, one of the most fragile, inchoate and evanescent of psychic states, is why one artist is valued over another and why a personal stamp will always be necessary. Without it universal truths are lifeless and without colour.

There are limits, however, to imaginative transformation. In the early part of this century, Modernists showed the importance of quotation, collage and montage for widening the frames of reference and, in the 1980s, Post-Modernists showed the necessity for dialogic, intertextuality, appropriation, multivalence – or the multi-voiced discourse. A poetics that accepts both the ready-made and the artist's sensibility in some kind of dialogue is more interesting, especially in art forms such as architecture which have to accept moments of the impersonal and the cliched. Hence a tension between the voice of the artist and the standardised solution, the transforming sensibility and the dumb constraints of building.

If art is valued partly for the particular vision of the artist, then this may be more or less developed and codified. Codes, or languages of design, can come from anywhere, but the ones I have adapted originate partly in the abstract work done by Op artists of the 1960s and a poetics that comes from contemporary science. Historically we are at an exciting moment when we have made discoveries at all levels of the universe, from the microcosm of the atom and its uncanny wave motion, to the mesocosm of the earth, Gaia, and its self-organising patterns of strange attractors, to the macrocosm and its galactic walls and self-organisation through expansion and jumps. Everywhere we find wave forms, and so I have continued to transform them through fractals, solitons and the metamorphoses of plants and concrete shapes (figure 11). The wave forms shown here are just one inner language, that of stripes and undulations, alternating bands of energy, light and dark, and light waves – a landscape of waves (figure 12).

After having said all this one still asks 'why bother?'. There is no single answer, but rather a series of motives which are more or less conscious. Why do animals, such as dogs, spontaneously show such affection and happiness, or why, as the philosopher Santayana asked, do we have animal faith? There is a natural identification with the universe which precedes thought; sceptics, scientists, atheists, nihilists even want to identify with something bigger than their tiny ego and so an art extended out to the largest measure of all is quite inevitable. The universe as a single, creative, unfolding event provides the narrative and grounding for culture.

Note

1 Sir Isaiah Berlin, *The Sense of Reality: Studies in Ideas and Their History*, Henry Hardy (ed), Farrar, Straus and Giroux, New York, 1997.

Figure 9. *The Physics Garden with (right to left) models of the atom, Gaia and the universe. Wave-forms are evident at the largest and smallest level. The Gaian model shows the history of the earth spiralling down from the top and the sun's energy – at the base – increasing by 30 percent over this period, sustaining and threatening Gaia.*

Figure 10. *Equations which generate the universe: the greenhouse supports the 12 most fundamental laws which underlie the universe (designed with Paul Davies and Brookbrae).*

Figure 11. *The DNA Eye (under construction) – metamorphosis of black optically vibrating waves from thin straight to thick curve, eye to inner eye, illusions to seeing.*

Figure 12. *Wave fence gate. Different densities of mesh create interference patterns of light waves.*

Head gardener: Alistair Clark; blacksmith: John Gibson; models of atoms Gaia universe: Brookbrae; construction of mounds: Hugh Hastings; Joinery: Bobby Dixon

THEATRE GARDEN
RÜDIGER SCHÖTTLE

The History

The history of the Theatre Garden and Bestiary is just as much the history of an exhibition as the history of a garden. From 1979 Rüdiger Schöttle wrote a series of texts, which, gathered together under the title *Psychomachia*, are both the starting point and theoretical completion of the project. Out of this, a large and small version of the model garden has arisen. Using the same title ('Psychomachia' refers to medieval depictions of the struggles between the vices and virtues), both versions have been exhibited in various museums since around 1987-89. The historical-cultural basis of both versions is the presentation of a baroque garden-as-poetry, theatre, museum, and, not least, as symbol and actual site of political power.

For the small version of the Theatre Garden, Schöttle devised a fantasy landscape of ruins constructed out of sugar and glass which he installed across an ascending step-like arrangement of tables barely 20 metres square. In the model, paths and buildings, illuminated by a succession of projected transparencies, are populated by numerous tin figures in historical costume. There are two ways in which observers can appropriate the exhibit. They can climb on to the viewing platforms on either side of the model, or wend their way through the garden along the tables, which are at roughly chest height.

Both means of experiencing the model are also integral to the large version, which has been on permanent display at the Château d'Oiron in France since 1992. For its first presentation in 1989 at New York's P.S.1 gallery, 13 artists developed their own individual perspectives on Schöttle's concept. New archetypes, such as Jeff Walls' baroque theatre and Dan Graham's cinema theatre, highlighted the power manifest in historic garden architectures and simultaneously drew on almost forgotten forms of theatre. Other contributions were devoted to the exhibitory aspect of the Theatre Garden, thematicising the exchanges between organiser, curator, artist, observer and art object. *(Susanne Prinz)*

Grosses Bestiarium, *1989*

The Theatre Garden and Bestiary

The Theatre Garden and Bestiary is an exhibition design that thematises our contemporary concept of autonomy.

In earlier times, things were collected into conglomerates. We were united by wonders, by strokes of good fortune – an idea which now appears as a singularity.

Within art, the particular refers to the framework – a horizon of events which, as a concept of autonomy, becomes the theme. Gravitational fields, that transfer adoption and object into definite states of movement, movements which are integrated into a general vector of time.

When we go to the cinema it is the bright surface that leaves us in darkness. We look into a mirror but see only the Other. The spectator is determined by his imagination, by the projected Other. A machinery sets our imaginings in motion.

This is an order which in the Theatre Garden is no longer that of Light-Dark. The recipients become the surface that is set in motion. They are no longer in the dark room, but are actually on those surfaces where events happen – the surfaces that mutually revolve round each other.

One finds oneself within a system of identities, which emerges out of the relationship of the individual with himself as an Other. The self reveals itself as a horizon as much as a singularity. What is projected here are social identities – mutualities that are translated back into individual identities.

In the Theatre Garden the art works are arranged on horizontal surfaces. Covered with reflective crystal, images appear on the surface that illuminate the exhibition space. Spectators can either sit on viewing platforms or they can wander among the projections. It is a horizontal cinema with several

Kleines Bestiarium, *1987, detail*

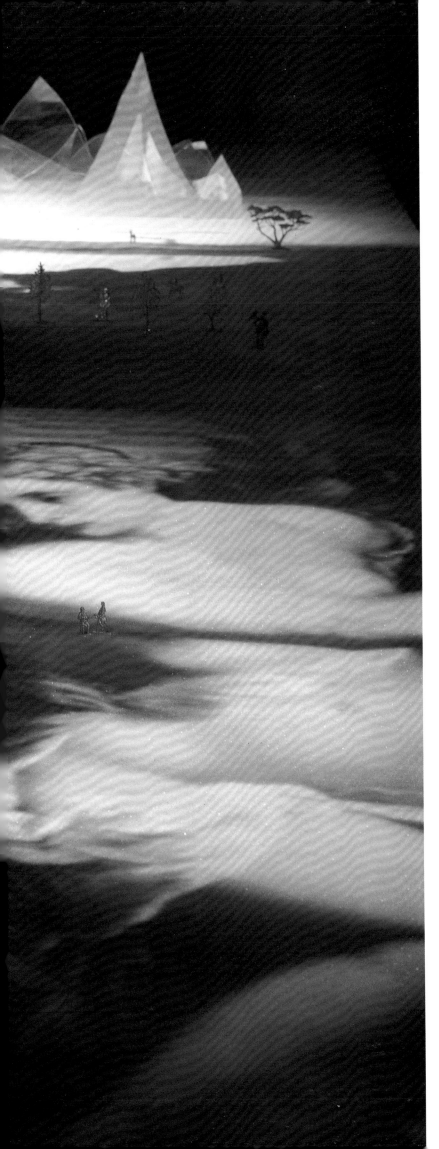

vanishing points and a contingent theory of combinations. Every moment gives rise to something new.

In the design of this garden the artists' contributions obey a combination field that transforms the spectator into his identity.

In the first version of the garden, the place of the artists' works is taken by a landscape of glass, sugar and figures – so that the Theatre Garden becomes a type of animated time-machine.

(*Rüdiger Schöttle*)

Kleines Bestiarium, *1987, detail*

Le jardin argenté, Parc André Citroën, 1990, Paris (photo Charles Chesshire)

CHANGING THE MYTH

An interview with Anne de Charmant

GILLES CLÉMENT

Anne de Charmant As a *paysagiste*[1] you seem to refute the status of artist for yourself when you say that your work cannot be compared to that of an architect or an artist because it involves an interaction with nature so significant that it amounts to a collaboration.

Gilles Clément Most of the time I do consider my work to be 'unsigned' as it only starts to live once it is out of my hands. A building, painting or sculpture tend not to evolve and live a life of their own, which is exactly the opposite of what happens to my gardens. Of course this is more or less true according to the proportion of 'nature' present in each garden. But it is especially true for my *jardins en mouvement*[2], in these cases I leave almost all initiative to nature – as well as to the gardener or caretaker who will guide the garden in its future life. The *jardin en mouvement* of the Parc André Citroën, near Paris, is being reseeded at present for the first time since its creation seven years ago. The decision was made to go back to the slightly more spectacular flowering of the original colonies. But, although I am kept informed, I am not in charge.

AdC Is there still 'art' in this shared authorship with nature?
GC There is certainly a call for a special understanding, a specific awareness of the processes of evolution and transformation so that there can be a reinterpretation. At its best a garden is a piece of nature interpreted for the enjoyment of man. It is an encounter between man and nature, a very privileged encounter. A garden is also the dwelling of utopia and of dreams, and all manner of things can happen there. It is where there is innocence and freedom from the prohibitions of society; a place of maximum enjoyment through an accumulation of 'bests' (the best flowers, the best fruits etc).

AdC This sounds like a definition of paradise. Is there a shift in the way we refer to Paradise and Arcadia in the context of the garden?
GC The image of the garden as metaphor for Paradise is definitely changing. At least in its opposition to Hell. For many centuries Paradise as mirrored by the garden was an ideal of order and calm imposed over the 'Hell' of the unadulterated wilderness. But these two notions are not as systematically opposed any more and actually haven't been for many years. Ecology has permeated our society and we tend to see things very differently. Nature is not the enemy any more and I believe we need to change our mythologies accordingly.

AdC In terms of gardens, this would then mean the triumph of the wild meadow or even the *friche*[3].
GC It would, and does, at least imply an acceptance of the natural process. Man will always need to mark his territory but in my mind he will increasingly do so in a spirit of toleration of nature and in collaboration with her own intrinsic mechanisms. We can do this today because we understand so much more about the interactions in the various small microcosms we inhabit and we are also starting to understand how this relates to a macrocosm. I believe a very important cultural phenomenon is presently at work deep in our collective psyche. One day we will wake up and realise we have new beliefs, new symbols. In this new system we will also have new tools and these will help us tend the planet as a garden. This is what I call the 'planetary garden' concept which is based on the notion of responsibility; an understanding of ecological finiteness leads to the realisation that the garden fence has moved beyond the traditional boundaries, to the planet and the biosphere. Man is responsible for the management of his planetary garden, in accordance with its fragility and its limits.

AdC Are you close to the German Green movement in gardens and landscape which advocates strict ecological principles?
GC I feel both very close and quite removed from it. I do not share the ecological radicalism and I am more open to planetary intermixing. It is hard for me to believe in a biological national landscape – there might be some native entities but they do not necessarily make biological sense. When I gave a talk in Germany last year there was a lot of interest in my ideas but professionals felt they could never be applied there as they involved too much openness in terms of species. There are many rules and obligations there which I cannot subscribe to; plants don't recognise boundaries and limits and nor do I.

AdC What about the English influence?
GC I admire immensely someone like the Irishman William Robinson [1838-1935], who brought on a total revolution in garden history, not only with his realisations, but with his writings and his research. However, his system and the style he advocated still separated man from nature. Unless one is the gardener, the professional, one still can't penetrate into the planting, walk amidst a mixed border and I believe in an immersion of man into the garden. Even with Robinson, the garden is still a representation, a spectacle and from there

Le Jardin des Simples, 1993, Blois

Parc André Citroën, 1990, Paris

La Vallée, Creuse

stems a danger of seeing a plant as a curious and precious object which one cares for just as one dusts and polishes trinkets on a mantelpiece. This is of course not at all what Robinson had in mind, but in England a lot of gardeners are more interested in collecting than in anything else. In many ways I admire this extraordinary variety, there is nothing I like more than pouring over endless plant lists from English suppliers. But I believe in gardens serving an idea, whereas in England the emphasis is more on decoration and performance.

AdC But these two definitions are so distant.

GC We are maybe talking about two different things; it is an interesting concept. But if one still believes that a garden is about utopia, then I would say that on this level, the English garden today, apart from a few exceptions, is in slight withdrawal. There is also the matter of fact approach of the English and I see it with my young English students. When I give them a case study, they will derive form from the pre-existent given of the terrain or other such considerations, instead of looking for a formal principle or concept into which one could integrate the constraints of the terrain. It is a diametrically opposed approach.

AdC Your own gardens are often culturally defined in the French tradition of the formal garden, which in many ways is the antithesis of your philosophies.

GC It is true that I am culturally anchored in a classical tradition; it is a pressure I cannot and do not want to escape. I respond to environments, and when I deal with an 18th-century facade, I respond in adequate, strong lines that will enhance the building. In my own garden at La Vallée, I combine various influences – English, Oriental, native – with different management techniques. I weed, prune and clip but I also apply the *jardin en mouvement* techniques depending on the space I have created, which itself is dictated by the environment.

AdC With projects like the Parc André Citroën, which you elaborated with Patrick Berger and Alain Provost, there is first and foremost a very strong abstract concept.

GC Throughout history, the garden has always been at the service of an idea, it always tells a story. And in the same way Citroën can be seen as a manifesto for the 20th century. My only regret is that I wasn't able to develop the *jardin en mouvement* on as big a scale as I had wished, but it appears to work as it is, which is proved by the numbers of visitors.

AdC How do you explain the new found passion of the French for the art of gardens?

GC After the war, the French became very interested in public spaces and parks but the private garden was considered as unworthy of much attention both by the profession and the public. Then came a key moment when the great historical gardens, which were still in private ownership, needed the help of the state and as a result were opened to the public. Special schemes were put into place by the architects and planners. Gradually the importance of gardens in French culture, as well as their great symbolic powers, was rediscovered. There were also quite a few designers and artists who had been thinking in terms of a renaissance of the art of the garden whether private or public. Eventually, about ten years ago, the French public started to develop an interest in horticulture, something from which they had previously been completely divorced. There had been a brief period of French horticultural excellence between the wars, around Tours and Nancy with extraordinary plantsmen, but all this had sunk into oblivion. Interest in horticulture has been revived through plant fairs like Courson and it is now an incredibly important market. At the same time a group of designers started thinking about new concepts and began to create gardens that were quite unique in Europe.

AdC There had to be a political will behind these realisations.

GC Not really, as always, political power follows a more widespread demand. But it is true that often local authorities were instrumental in these developments, as was the Mairie of Paris for the Parc André Citroën and Bercy. To me, the Parc de la Villette was a key realisation in the recent history of French gardens – although La Villette is not a garden as such but a collection of small gardens and recreational exhibition spaces – it also has been very important in terms of a new place for the public.

AdC It gave rise to a lot of criticism because of the radically abstract overall design.

GC Yes it gave rise to an interesting debate. There was a slight provocation behind Bernard Tschumi's system of follies which it is quite abstract and difficult to grasp. But despite that there is at once both a canvas and a looseness that enable the whole system to function well. The Parc has evolved in terms of its public usage and it opened the way for many other such projects.

Notes

1 The French word *paysagiste* for landscape or garden designer literally means 'landscaper'.

2 Gilles Clément developed the concept of *jardin en mouvement* (garden in motion) from experiments carried out in his own garden of La Vallée. It amounts to a managed system of seeded and existing

meadow where all plants 'good' or 'bad' are allowed to spread, mingle or even disappear.

3 The notion of *friche* (fallow land) is understood by Clément as excluding both nature and culture as it is 'abandoned' land colonised by all manner of imported as well as native species.

Itsuko Hasegawa, Shonandai Cultural Centre, 1989, Fujizawa (photo Günter Nitschke)

JAPANESE CONTEMPORARY GARDENS: A SENSE OF UNITY

An Interview with Charles Chesshire

GÜNTER NITSCHKE

Charles Chesshire In 1968 Lorraine Kluck ended her book *Japanese Gardens* with the comment that the use of natural rocks to create designs would become recognised as one of the world's important art forms. Recently I saw Shodo Susuki's work 'Archipelago' at the garden festival at Chaumont-sur-Loire in France. He had natural rocks laid out in a traditional manner in the pattern of the Japanese archipelago itself. The tops of the stones had been sliced off horizontally and polished smooth. I believe Susuki saw this as representing the dilemmas facing modern-day Japan with its increasing disconnection from nature. His creations are instantly recognisable as Japanese and the same is true of the work of many prominent Japanese designers of recent years such as Susuki and Moto Yoshimura and artists like Mirei Shigemori and Isamu Noguchi. Why do you think this is so?

Günter Nitschke The fact that one unmistakably recognises a garden by a Japanese designer, even in our day, probably has something to do with the fact that even the most modern Japanese designer is less alienated from nature and its mysteries than a Western designer.

CC Is this also because what we call 'abstraction' in the West has always been present in Japan, even in a garden like the Ryoanji, built in the late 1400s?

GN All gardens are man-made and are therefore abstractions of nature. The abstraction is simply a matter of degree. In the Japanese cultural context the composition of the Ryoanji was probably the climax of abstraction reached in Japanese gardening. In that sense it appeals to the Western eye. To me its most complete reinterpretation is Noguchi's sunken court-yard in front of the Rare Books Library at Yale University in the 1960s. It somehow melts the abstract formal language of the anonymous and nature-affirming garden of Ryoanji with the individual-as-artist represented by Noguchi. As he mentioned in an interview shortly before his death in 1989, 'The garden is made from a collaboration with nature. Man's hands are hidden by time and by many effects of nature, moss and so forth, so you are hidden. I don't want to be hidden. I want to show. Therefore I am modern. I am not a traditionalist *Ueki-ya*, tree trimmer.' But it must be said that in Japan, Noguchi, who was half American and spent most of his life there, had little influence on garden design.

CC Both you and Lorraine Kluck refer to the work of Mirei Shigemori as the key figure in shaking up what had become, by the 1930s, a stagnating art form.

GN Yes, and this is best illustrated in Shigemori's garden Tofukuji, which forms the moment of transition from the stereotypical reproduction of traditional garden themes and scenery, to the modern prototype of the garden, that steps into the unknown, where the gardener functions effectively as sculptor. It marks the start of a new relationship between man and garden, between the creator and the created. Stone carving, though previously seen in lanterns, stepping stones and water basins, had never been hewn into sculptural forms and then combined in decorative compositions.

CC It was Shigemori who helped to bring the mystique of the gardens of the Ryoanji and the other dry, minimalist temple gardens to the fore, but in a new form.

GN Shigemori and Kenzo Tange are the two most powerful and creative instigators of the final and modern prototype of the Japanese garden, representing 'mindscapes'. Yes, Shigemori more or less single-handedly forced the 'sacred' dry land-scape out of hiding in Buddhist temple precincts.

But it was Kenzo Tange who extracted the last taste of Zen out of the minimalist garden with his design for the Kagawa Prefectural Offices in Takamatsu (1958). Here the natural rock was finally killed as an object of beauty as the tree was 30 years later in the 'Cool Garden' by Hiroshi Murai. Tange completely eliminated the notion of raked sand which had to be attended to every day. He freed the Japanese from the *soji no jigoku,* Hells of Cleaning, as Buddhist temples were referred to in Zen circles because of their obsession with cleaning. Tange substituted real water for the raked sand.

CC What would you describe as the greatest influence in Japan today?

GN After Noguchi's version at Yale, the Ryoanji seems to have run out of steam as a model and inspiration. In a way one would really like to exclaim with Nietzsche that 'God is dead and man is free'. What the Orders were to architecture surely Ryoanji must have been to garden design. But, to return to your earlier question, whether the untouched natural rock will become the star of the modern garden, yes, perhaps but only in the West. In Japan it will be the cut rock, at least for a while. But I believe that the garden of the future will suggest some-thing like a jungle. A garden created as a jungle could be as

The Ryoanji Garden, Kyoto, c1490 (photo Günter Nitschke)

Mirei Shigemori, Yuzen Kimono Dyeing Union Headquarters, Kyoto, 1975 (photo Günter Nitschke)

Moss and Stone Garden, Kyoto (photo Christopher Jones)

influential an image of our attitude towards nature now, as a garden created for aesthetic pleasure was a thousand years ago: an image of our attitude towards culture.

CC About the use of synthetic materials in Japanese garden design, you say that metal and plastic, although not 'ready-mades' of nature, may still count as natural materials.

GN Metal and plastic as materials for rock formations have become a common sight in Japan. And I believe that metal and plastic are definitely part of nature but they are only beautiful as long as they appear as they are. Why do the sheet-metal trees or the winding river of plastic tiles in Itsuko Hagesawa's Shonondai Cultural Centre (1989) have to imitate the natural form of trees or rivulets? I do not understand why the now famous 'second nature' of Hasegawa has simply imitated 'first nature'. For this reason Arakawa and Madeline Gin's 'Gardens of Reversible Destiny' do not reverse our human destiny but make it more interesting because their forms are purely those of a 'mindscape'.

CC What makes up contemporary attitudes to landscape and garden design in Japan today?

GN At least three different attitudes have emerged over the last 20 years. The most recent and maybe the more publicised one is the grand and slightly sterile approach of architects trained at Western-style universities who are well established on the international scene. The second one is a more classical approach, deeply rooted in the rich Japanese tradition of garden design which in some cases amounts to plain imitation. And then there is a more original way which combines traditional roots with contemporary architecture and design. I would mention here the works of Nakane Shiro who worked for over 40 years with his father very much in a traditionally inspired style, but who now designs for architects such as Emilio Ambasz in a much more progressive style. There is also the more ecologically minded approach of those like Moto Yoshimura who has been given the mandate of restoring the exhibition site of the Osaka exhibition ground. He speaks of restoration and harmony but he feeds very much on traditional values in design and architecture.

CC In your book *Japanese Gardens* [Taschen 1991] you wrote of the new gardens which use carved rock as the main compositional element with geometry as the spatial infrastructure stating that this new prototype is not a mirror of nature, neither in its outer appearance nor in its inner mode of operation. You have termed them 'mindscapes' since they are not found in nature but are products of the human imagination. Does this suggest a superiority of the artist over nature, rather than an intimacy?

GN The most recent example of that type of garden making and certainly the most publicised is that by Peter Walker and

Arata Isozaki at the Tokyo Marine Training Centre and also their Centre for Advanced Science and Technology in Ilyogo Prefecture. This type of garden, which has come to be symbolic of 'high culture' in Japan, contains a modern sterile world of geometric patterns where Walker has used line as a metaphor of Japan's agricultural past. Obviously there were rice fields, but to impose such an abstract view of nature and 'mindscape' onto nature I find perverse. Nature will do everything to destroy those lines. To me, this reliance on geometry as a prime landscape design principle in this case indicates a boredom with and disinterest in nature's own intrinsic complexity and beauty.

CC You finished your last book on Japanese gardens with 'meditation' as your mantra for hope, for healing the rift between Man and nature. This is a great inspiration for many of us in the West, and is what gives the Japanese garden the ultimate ability to transcend the mundane and material world. To many it is an elusive and stark image but one that surely must still have great importance in Japan.

GN To me it is, or should be, an extremely important part of garden design. But it is one that tends to be overlooked by practitioners today. Although I am not alone in being aware of ecological systems, I believe that one can induce an experience of the unity of nature and awaken the sense of being a man in nature through design. But in order to do that one has to live in an extreme state of awareness and live and act accordingly. Simple intellectual or scientific knowledge of the interdependence of all life forms on this globe will not reduce the pollution, as our recent past teaches us. We know one thing and act in opposition to it. Meditation can function as a healing therapy.

CC Is it possible for designers who are living in this state of awareness to transfer that experience through their designs to the viewer, so that the viewer may feel even just a little of that serenity? Is this what the Zen masters hoped for or was this for their own experience only?

GN Meditation induces an experience that is far from being serene in the sense that tends to mean boring and meant only for bloodless saints. Instead it is utterly ecstatic. It is something of a 'Silent Orgasm' (the title of my recent book) [Taschen 1995]. The sense of separateness of the ego is serene and serious and the experience of ego-death the ultimate ecstasy. It makes you realise that everything in nature enjoys ecstatic union constantly. Designing with that awareness of wholeness becomes healing for oneself and for nature.

CC Have you seen this anywhere?

GN I have seen this very rarely and when it has been achieved it has not been published. I have, however, found no record in the literature of Zen Buddhism or of gardening that even speaks

Hiroshi Murai, Cool Garden, 1972, Longchamp Textile Company, Kyoto (photo Günter Nitschke)

of a possible transfer of the experience of this sense of unity and ecstasy from master to disciple by means of design. Nor is there any record of anyone becoming enlightened by simply looking at a garden.

The dry landscape gardens, mostly attached to priests' living quarters from the 15th century onwards, were basically introduced to the West as 'meditation gardens' by the first generation of Zen interpreters (not Zen masters by the way). Meditation however was practised in special halls with no view outside while the garden was simply a translation of the 12th-century Chinese Song Dynasty monochrome landscape painting into three dimensions, and viewed like a painting from a fixed vantage point. No, the real link to Zen lies in the daily practice of attending to the gardens, the rituals, just as it is with brush painting or the tea ceremony. I say this but from my own experiments with the Ryoanji, I feel it may well have been used for meditation.

CC So if you believe this sense of unity can be recreated, who

of any of the contemporary designers have attained this?

GN Truth, beauty and unity cannot be hidden forever. They wait to be revealed. They have to be constantly rediscovered and recreated. The Buddhist temple precinct can still be a source for new and truly creative design, as shown by two examples, both by the architect Tadao Ando. One is the water lawn garden of the Chapel-on-the-Water at Tomamu, Hokkaido (1988), and the other is the lotus pond garden of the Hompukuji Water Temple on Awajishima Island (1991). Both defy categories such as modern, traditional, Japanese or Western and both are completely unique new forms of garden. Their attraction lies in their ability to transmit to us a sense of unity with nature, they make us larger just as all true art does.

CC Does this sense of hope also exist in ordinary life away from the secret life of temples, or must it come from the artist or the professionals?

GN Probably not through the academic or the artist, though the artist is obviously the most finely-tuned receptacle. Yes, I

Masamichi Suzuki, Hotel Sheraton Grande on Tokyo Bay, 1988 (photo Günter Nitschke)

do see hope in ordinary life. In ordinary life in Japan, people are quite attuned to nature. In my little village near Kyoto each autumn there is a big poster displayed in the railway station with a list of over 20 famous gardens. The station master calls around the gardens every day to know the exact state of the reddening of the maples. When the garden is ready he pins up a maple leaf in one of five boxes next to the name of each garden according to five categories of 'redness'. In the spring it is the same with the cherry blossoms. I see this hope more in the reaction to over-urbanisation among the average Japanese.

CC What effect will nature have, if anything, on something like the 'Cool Garden'? Will the modern Japanese allow something like the 'Cool Garden' to grow moss around it for us to contemplate in another 500 years, just as they have with the Ryoanji?
GN No, I think the Japanese will just destroy them. The 'Cool Garden' has very much the quality of a temporary installation

rather than a piece of eternal art. One doesn't believe in the city eternal and beautiful in Japan but in the city vital and ever changing. They will just pull it down one day. It happens to me constantly in Kyoto that I make a date somewhere and I go there and it has been pulled down. We imagine that the Japanese have a lot of problems which in fact they don't have. Because we in the West live with this ontological dichotomy of God/world, spirit/matter, man/nature, body/soul, we attribute to them a much more complex relationship with nature than they actually have. They don't see themselves in such an unhappy situation as we see ourselves.

CC So they don't have the same guilt that we have towards the environment?
GN No, they don't. When something gets destroyed by man it is to them as if a typhoon ran through it or a fire. This attitude still exists. A friend once said to me, 'the Japanese don't have a problem with nature because they see themselves as nature'.

'TO SEE THE WORLD IN A GRAIN OF SAND'[1]

Paradise Found in Derek Jarman's Dungeness Garden

STEPHANIE WATSON

Houses can be seen as mirrors of the psyche through which we access the world as it accesses us in return, until we choose to close our eyes or turn away our gaze – what then, metaphorically speaking, is a garden?

A garden acts as a meeting point between our private gaze and public inspection, an open environment where our relationship to the world is defined. Gardens come in many shapes and forms, mirroring the variety of people who create them. They are assimilations between the natural environment and human intervention, in symbolic terms – pre-Fall, and post-Fall, Eden. Gardens can be paradises, wildernesses, status symbols, conformist, escapist, formal, 'artificial', spiritual, functional, secluded, private, public, untended, and so on according to personal taste.

Derek Jarman's garden surrounding his wooden fisherman's cottage, on the shingle formation of Dungeness, is an extraordinary place of contradiction, variety and atmospheric freedom, it enchants the visitors who explore and admire it. Dungeness is a bleak, working, and often harsh environment for growing plants. It is a triangular stretch of land lying on the tip of Kent and is bordered by the sea on two sides. Dungeness seems to have a separate weather pattern from the inland

area. It also has very clear and luminescent light which makes the colours of the beach appear surprisingly vivid. Dungeness is a registered Site of Special Scientific Interest because of its indigenous plant species, particulary its rare lichens. Jarman bought Prospect Cottage in 1987 and gradually began to create a garden. Sculptures of stone and driftwood were soon joined by a wide variety of plants, many of which appear to be symbolic, evoking Jarman's personal experiences of life, his work, political stances and gardening, alongside mythical, traditional, pharmaceutical and folklore interests. It is an unique garden where definitions are broken down and blended on many levels.

Jarman's garden is divided fairly equally between the front and the back of the cottage. The back meets a wide tract of land, dominated by the grey cuboid chunks of the nuclear power station to the left, while the green 'garden' of Kent can be glimpsed to the right, enclosing the tip of an ancient church steeple buried in trees. This landscape of gorse and pebble, with its scattered telegraph poles and more distant pylons is a wilderness reminiscent of industrial, and First World War wastelands. The garden runs both sides of the cottage, where neighbouring cottages exist in fairly close proximity yet do not have

noticeable hedges, walls or fences. The front, which faces the rising sun and the beach next to the sea, is suggestive of Edward Hopper's Cape Cod paintings. The front of the garden is subtly bordered by a small and basic road which runs through the Dungeness estate to the nuclear power station, past small businesses serving the fishing industry, evidenced by the fishing huts, boats and machinery near the sea; a pub, two lighthouses (one striped like a zebra crossing); a cafe, and a small rail terminal serving the Romney, Hythe and Dymchurch railway line, whose miniature trains blow puffs of steam as they traverse the land between Jarman's cottage and the power station. It is a surreal environment.

Jarman's garden does not have formal boundaries, it echoes and merges into the surrounding landscape of pebble interspersed with patches of coarse grass, seakale and gorse. In common with Jarman's work, a process has taken place within the garden where internal exploration has been opened out and positioned in its relationship to the external world, Jarman stated that is the 'the attrition point, and that's what makes Art'.[2] Jarman's work often engaged with an 'alchemical' transformation of past traditions and modern sensibilities, aware that rigid definitions, interpretations and boundaries, both in

representational forms and life itself, are often repressive – hypocritical authorities which seek to capture and exclude individual experiences which oppose or evade their rules. Gardens offer constant change and transformation, where, within the context of continuity, of renewal and seasonal return, plants naturally tend to expand their boundaries, mingling with each other and exhibiting a 'shaggy' quality which Jarman found so attractive in Monet's garden at Giverny. Jarman's life and work also expanded boundaries, providing public and open access as he moved between autobiography, writing, filmmaking, and painting, often combining one medium with another, and embodying his work with political, as well as aesthetic, functions. Jarman's garden occupies a symbolic space where the personal as well as the English identity are reworked.

The garden threads through Jarman's journals, paintings, and films, and is referenced in visual, poetic, historical, cultural, mythological and personal terms. Often these references evoke a nostalgia for a 'lost paradise', or a respect for the diversity of the natural landscape (social and visual), prior to the arrival of Thatcherism, Clause 28 and a 'theme-park' approach to tradition and the countryside. Jarman believed that his garden was haunted by paradise, 'Like all true

gardeners, I am an optimist',[3] and identified with, amongst others, 'Blake and William Morris . . . all of them look backward over their shoulders – to a paradise on earth. And all of them at odds with the world around them.'[4] His film *The Garden* (1990) presents the garden in actual and symbolic terms as a place of transformation where the Judao-Christian accounts of the Fall from Eden, Christ's flight from Herod, and the Crucifixion, are reworked to represent persecution by the empty morality of the media gaze. Jarman's work does not oppose 'mainstream' culture, it merely reveals that the 'mainstream' and the 'marginal' have an interdependent history, and that their supposed opposition is arbitrary. *Derek Jarman's Garden* (Thames & Hudson, with photographs by Howard Sooley) combines various literary genres (autobiography, poetry, and documentary) to provide a very evocative and beautiful account of the garden, and has a popular and diverse appeal because it communicates a positive desire to transform our environment.

The garden's lack of formal boundaries and its pebble form make it appear to stretch to the horizon, as one perplexed visitor observed, 'it's like being on the beach'. The variety of planting and atmosphere is surprising, and is emphasised by the sculptures, smells and sounds. The garden evokes such seeming contradictions as the Japanese meditational garden and the traditional cottage garden with its yew trees and random mixture of herbs, flowers, and indigenous plants, such as the seakale which returns each year, changing from purple to green, producing white flowers, and green 'pea' seeds, before being bleached by the sun and blown away by the harsh sea wind. The garden can roughly be divided into two separate areas, the front is formal and low-lying, whilst the back is more random, incorporating vertical sculptures made from pieces of found driftwood and metal. The larger, more imposing sculptures are made of functional, 'crafted' wood (such as ship beams) and appear totemic; they stand in circles of gorse containing concentric pebble 'ripples' on the outskirts of the garden. The smaller sculptures tend to use more natural wood or metal structures such as twisted coil pyramids. Wood and metal are often combined together to serve practical as well as aesthetic functions, supporting or marking plants, often decorated on top by a single, or chain of 'holey' stones, or beneath by a circle of cork pieces. Tools and found objects, washed up onto the beach, or used in the garden's construction also add sculptural effect; lifebuoys, spades, lamps and so on. Some of these sculptures are in crucifix form, such as two crossed pipes and a piece of driftwood transversed by a metal spanner. This inclusion of found objects expresses a Beat sensibility towards transforming and finding beauty or meaning in everyday objects which have been consigned to more mundane functions.

The metal sculptures create sound, especially two which are decorated with metal triangles, reminiscent of the fishing boats. Amongst the buzz of the power station (if the wind is calm), the birds which whistle and dart amongst the pebbles can also be heard, along with the booming foghorn on days when the entire landscape becomes obscured – yet overall the garden is very peaceful. Smell is created particularly by the santolinas and herbs, which form bushy and subtle spherical shapes, contrasting with vertical red hot pokers, mallows, and thistle plants. Winding pebble paths move between the sculptures and plants. The vertical shapes complement the spherical forms creating open compartments offering enclosure and space; they also create a continuity with the environment by echoing the telegraph poles and pylons. The back garden contrasts detail and sculptural pattern. It also emphasises the relationship between the man-made environment and nature, which is seen as one of opposition, support and interchange.

To the west of Prospect Cottage lies an old wooden fishing boat, whilst to the south side of the cottage, a large vertical beam is centred inside a formal horizontal square of wooden beams with a further square inside. On the south wall, cut-out wooden letters in Jarman's handwriting present a verse from John Donne's poem, 'The Sunne Rising'. The text is partially obscured by the weathering that it received before the cottage was painted with protective black tar varnish, and by its original spelling. This emphasises the limited power of boundaries and definitions.

> Busie old foole, unruly Sunne,
> Why dost thou thus,
> Through windowes, and through curtaines call on us?
> Must to thy motions lovers' seasons run?
> Sawcy pedantique wretch, goe chide
> Late schoole boyes and sowre prentices,
> Goe tell Court-huntsmen, that the King will ride,
> Call country ants to harvest offices;
> Love, all alike, no season knowes, nor clyme,
> Nor houres, dayes, moneths, which are the rags of time . . .
> Thou sunne art halfe as happy as wee,
> In that the world's contracted thus.
> Thine age askes ease, and since thy duties bee
> To warme the world that's done in warming us.
> Shine here to us, and thou art every where;
> This thy bed is, these walls thy spheare.

The poem chides the sun for the conceit of attempting to define and measure out warmth, when another form of warmth exists, unlimited by the hours of the day or seasons – love. The external positioning of the poem on the boundary of the cottage and the garden, emphasises the blurring of the boundary between internal vision and the world outside, illustrating that gardens can be places of transgression and freedom.

The front garden is composed mainly of large, circular flint and pebble beds (the outer grey flint borders are standing), which are colour differentiated. These beds contain a variety of plants, poppies, santolinas and marigolds, amongst

(photos Gillian Watson)

others. Three beds lead up towards the house from the road, the first is grey and contains a wind clipped yew. The second is oblong, framed grey with white pebbles enclosing a circle of red and grey pebbles. Whilst the bed in front of the house is composed of alternating circles of driftwood and flint. These beds are ablaze with colour in mid-summer (Jarman dug them out and filled the beds with manure). The effect is formal yet vibrant as the stones bring their own colour.

Reactions to Jarman's garden vary: some hesitate to intrude and stand by the roadside, a few storm in like curio hunters, picking up stones and peering through windows; some reflect, while others quickly survey. Some think the garden follows classical traditions of design, others oppose this view, praising its unconventional originality, some onlookers are simply perplexed or surprised that the garden is so public, so near to other houses and Dungeness 'features'. Like Shakespeare's more ambiguous and 'open' texts, such as *The Tempest*, Jarman's garden allows us to add our own personal feelings and interpretations. The garden is exciting to visit, combining older garden sensibilities with new surprises and discoveries. Most visitors respect its accessibility, often returning to observe the changing seasons, and the garden's evolution by those who tend it and continue Jarman's work.

Returning to the question of what a garden is: Derek Jarman's garden is a generous expression of the relationship between internal vision and the external world. Some have suggested that it, and gardening in general, represent an escapist activity beyond the reaches of social concerns. Gardening does present the chance to lose oneself, yet this pleasure can also acknowledge confrontation with the outside world. Jarman's work, particularly his later work which openly confronted homophobia, media 'scares' and personal experience concerning the HIV virus and AIDS, is largely autobiographical and accessible. Politics is about opposition, confrontation and hidden alliances. Jarman's garden deals with all of these, accepting confrontation, exposing and uniting contradiction, both in physical terms and within the larger part they played in Jarman's outlook on life. Perhaps this sense of freedom, of a new way of viewing convention without reproduction or escapism is what appeals to visitors, the majority of whom respect the accessibility of the garden. As Jarman stated, 'I am useful because I'm showing people how to do it for themselves. That's the most important thing anyone can discover. Themself. So in that sense art is vital and does contribute.'[5]

Notes

1 From William Blake, *Auguries of Youth*.

2 Derek Jarman quoted in, 'Through a Screen Darkly', *Rapid Eye*, Simon Dwyer (ed), Creation Books, London, 1995 (first pub 1989), p259.

3 *The Last of England*, David Hirst (ed), Constable, London, 1987, p151.

4 *Modern Nature: The Journals of Derek Jarman*, Vintage, London, 1987, p151.

5 *Ibid*, p273.

CHAUMONT: A FESTIVAL OF EXPERIMENTS

The Château de Chaumont-sur-Loire, situated high up on the banks of the Loire between Blois and Amboise is one of the jewels on the circuit of the châteaux of the Loire Valley. Atypically, it stands on grounds that were landscaped in the 'English style' during the 19th century in the epidemic that transformed many of mainland Europe's gardens into 'romantic parks'. Since 1992, however, the park of Chaumont has been a centre of activity and experimentation devoted to the garden of the 21st century. The Festival International des Jardins was created at the initiative of the Région Centre and has since taken place every year, attracting over 450,000 visitors. In an area of around three hectares of the park, the celebrated Belgian designer Jacques Wirtz devised a pattern of 30 individual spaces of approximately 250 metres square, each enclosed by beech hedges. In itself this system of small gardens delineates a rambling plant or a bouquet. In the first year, 30 landscape designers and artists from around the world were each invited to create an experimental garden. Most spaces have a new occupant every year but some gardens were so successful, or so perfectly established, or even so architecturally coherent, that it was decided to maintain them. This was the case for example with Patrice Blanc's 'vegetal walls'. Here an intricate association of plants grows on almost horizontal walls, covered in a felt-like matting, on the surface of which plants are grown in small pockets. With water constantly streaming down the face of the walls, the plants grow amazingly well and this project is so successful that it will soon be put into practice in Paris to create a number of vertical gardens. This development is typical of what happens in Chaumont where experiment and innovations are never gratuitous even if some creations are inevitably less interesting than others. Determined to favour practical applications, the festival is intricately linked to the Conservatoire International des Parcs et Jardins et du Paysage, which acts as a teaching and research centre as well as a publicly oriented centre of information and activities. The sixth year of the festival, in 1997, was themed around water.

(Anne de Charmant)

OPPOSITE: École Boulle, Ailleurs, 1996 (photo Mosaik); BELOW: Michèle Elsair and Jean-Pierre Delettre, Carrousel d'Eau, 1997 (photo Elsair/Delettre)

FROM ABOVE L TO R: Béatrice Fauny and Benoît Séjourné, Jardin d'ombre et d'ombrelles, 1996 (photo Mosaik/ B Coutier); Atelier de l'Entrepôt, La Volière, 1996 (photo Edouard François); Edouard François and Duncan Lewis, La Serre Molle, 1996 (photo Mosaik); Haruto Kobayashi, Le jardin des trois éléments, 1992-93 (photo Papyrus)

FROM ABOVE L TO R: Conservatoire de Chaumont, Le Baobab qui pleure, 1997 (photo Papyrus); Emilio Ambasz, Nymphée, 1995 (photo Mayer/Le Scanff); Markus Gnüchtel, Le Jardin du Petit Prince, 1996 (photo Perdereau); Hiroshi Teshigahara, 1992-93 (photo Papyrus)

FUTURE GARDEN

The Endangered Meadows of Europe

HELEN MAYER HARRISON, NEWTON HARRISON

You said
The meadow represents an old wisdom.
It is humble and unassuming.
Yet it is a vast cultural landscape
a sensual and pleasing many purposed landscape
constructed over millennia
an aesthetic that is no longer being remembered
an information ground that is rapidly being lost.

And you said
Imagine a new forest
constructed intentionally over time
with the meadow as a model.
So that this new forest
like the meadow will be a cultural construction
and will supply food for people and livestock
and wood and whatever
as well as cleansing waters and air.
Extracts from *Meadow Stories*, Text XV

The present work is one of the latest in a series of works with grasslands and meadows which began with a small indoor installation of a hog pasture at the Boston Museum of Fine Arts in 1971. It is also a work of representational sculpture, a continuously changing, living, colour field that covers about 3,600 square metres on the centre of the rooftop of the Kunst-und Ausstellungshalle der Bundesrepublik Deutschland, Bonn. The work sets out to transform the roof into a field on which a complex drama is acted out. The drama begins with the decision to save a 400-year-old meadow from the Eifel, a hilly region in former West Germany, transplanting it to the roof instead of letting it be torn up and replaced by a housing project. This decision sets the stage. Thereafter, sections of other endangered meadows, a wet meadow, a dry meadow and a stone meadow, are combined to make a diverse ensemble. A series of conversations between us, scientists and 'meadow masters', as it were, described the history and cultural function of meadows. Photographic images of meadows from other parts of Europe and certain fencing structures

Future Garden: Part I, *1996-98, Kunst-und Ausstellungshalle der Bundesrepublik Deutschland, Bonn (photos Heidrun Weiler and Peter Oszvald)*

all together confront and co-join, presenting this drama, a drama which unfolds when walking around the meadow perimeter.

This ecological narrative gives voice to a unique element in the European cultural landscape. The meadow lands of Europe are a recent phenomena from an ecological point of view. They have developed over several centuries as a result of forest clearance and are maintained in their present form by the grazing of livestock and/or the annual cutting of hay. This kind of agriculture is a mode of spontaneous and profitable, although unconscious, collaboration between man and nature. Cutting and grazing has set the stage for a meadow ecosystem in Europe of considerable complexity and stability, one of the most successful collaborative and sustainable ventures between humans and the rest of the ecosystem.

The intact meadow ecosystem supported microscopic life, invertebrates and insects, various plants, reptiles, amphibians, mammals and avians, as well as the livestock that grazed it and the farmers who mowed it and brought in the cows. It

was, in fact, the yearly cutting of the meadows that maintained the system and prevented the natural succession forest from returning. Thus, all participated in giving balance and stability to this specific ecosystem. Here the harvest preserved two systems, one cultural and the other ecological, each helpful to the other's well-being. This remarkable element in the cultural landscape is endangered in many parts of Europe by overcutting and overgrazing and mechanising agriculture so that, in the end, a biodiverse system becomes a monoculture.

Paradoxically, even as it is being destroyed and replaced the meadow as it has evolved is, and will continue to be, a valuable model for future survival. We see this collaborative model speaking across time, offering choices, posing questions and functioning as a potential model for future man–nature collaborations. Thinking about this we begin to imagine a future forest, a future estuary, a future lake. In fact, we imagine monoculture Europe transforming itself into a future garden, a biologically diverse system, with the meadow as the model.

Bernard Lassus, Jardin des Retours, Rochefort-sur-Mer, 1991

FROM LAND ART TO GARDEN LANDSCAPE

STEPHEN BANN

The aim of this essay is to sketch out a series of distinctions between three types of relationship which exist between 'art' and 'nature' at the present time. The points to be made are, on one level, reasonably obvious, but this clarification is necessary if we are to understand some of the confusions which underlie the theory and practice of landscape at the end of the 20th century.

The first area of consideration is the contemporary phenomenon of 'land art', for which the work of Richard Long serves as a specially clear index. The second will be the more generalised phenomenon of the 'sculpture park', as it has emerged in the post-war period and, especially, in the last 20 years. Particular references will be to the Villa Celle, near Pistoia in Tuscany, not because it is necessarily a typical example, but because it illustrates some of great potentialities as well as the limitations of the genre. The third area will take into account the garden pure and simple focusing on the work of two artists of the present day who have created – and who continue to create – gardens: the Scotsman Ian Hamilton Finlay and the Frenchman Bernard Lassus.

These three types of expression are not placed in any historical or evolutionary order. On the contrary, at first sight they appear to be linked by mutual antagonisms and contradictions. For example, the motivation of the land artist would appear to be deeply antagonistic to the concept of the sculpture park: the land artist has no wish to remain within the museum circuit, even that of the open air museum, but journeys to the ends of the earth. No less clearly, the practice of land art would seem to have little to do with the creation of gardens, which is a traditional practice, relying on artisan skill and experience; though of course there have always been gardener/architects who take it upon themselves to move mountains.

In parenthesis, it is interesting to consider one exception which proves this rule. There can be no doubt that Robert Smithson, the great pioneer of land art in the American and world-wide domain, well understood the potential link between his own practice and that of the pioneer of American landscape and garden designers, Frederick Olmsted, whose parks adorn a great number of cities in the United States and Canada. Gilles Tiberghien has rightly reprinted in his book on land art a text by Smithson which discusses Olmsted's significance at length.[1] It is difficult to disagree with the analysis given by Smithson, in so far as he relates Olmsted's approach to the 'picturesque' tendency in English gardening, represented around 1800 by Uvedale Price and William Gilpin. Nor can it be denied that the Modernists – Ezra Pound and TS Eliot are among the names that Smithson cites – were concerned to eliminate the tradition of the picturesque from contemporary poetics, as a result of which the mutual enrichment of poetry and garden art characteristic of English culture since the 17th century ceased to take place. But even though Smithson sees these matters with great clarity in his writing on Olmsted, it is doubtful whether his own practice – curtailed by his early death – was able to alter or reverse the situation which he described.

My own hypothesis, which of course exists only to be tested, consists in three propositions relating to the different domains considered here. In the first place, I argue that land art is an art which is basically inseparable from the modernist tendency, in so far as it depends upon a specific tension between the space of exhibition and its 'other': in this case, the natural world. In the second place, I hold that the sculpture park is neither an art form, nor a garden, nor indeed a part of 'nature' in any significant sense. It is very precisely a museological development: one which gains its value and interest to the extent that it expands the museum's field without challenging the status of the exhibiting space as it has been established in the modern period.

The third category, the garden, should not be confused with land art, or the sculpture park, even though, from a phenomenological point of view, it can be difficult to make this distinction. The garden is an art form in itself. Thus it makes no sense to consider it as 'housing' sculpture or other exhibited objects in the way that a museum does. It is itself a total art work, and connotes a sequence of earlier total art works which flourished at least from the time of the Renaissance to the beginning of the modern epoch. But the garden is not just a historical throw-back; it is, in the present period, a completely contemporary project. Indeed it is a polemical project which exposes the formalist assumptions at the heart of much of the 'public art' being created at the present time. I am tempted to suggest that the garden is both a pre-modern and a post-modern mode of art.

I can immediately see the objections which could be made to this series of propositions. Surely Monet made a wonderful garden at Giverny, while remaining incontestably a major modern painter? I beg leave to differ here. In fact, it is doubtful whether Monet made a garden in any essential sense of the term. That

FROM ABOVE: David Nash, Sod Swap, 1983, Kensington Gardens, London; Bernard Lassus, Autoroute A 85 Angers-Tours, 1997; William Kent, stone channels at Rousham, Oxfordshire, c 1738 (photo Charles Chesshire)

is to say, he did a remarkable thing in setting up a significant relationship between the planted space, which developed over a number of years, and its representation on a plane surface: specifically a canvas of an area of some square centimetres. If you look at the Allée des Rosiers at Giverny (and this means catching it in late summer, when the flowering is at its height), you can appreciate that this alley was designed to be represented in two dimensions, in the form of a painting. Monet's celebrated waterlilies are, by contrast, to create a possibility of visual liaison between the sky and the specially created pond, in this way cancelling out any obvious spatial reference. But they can only achieve this effect fully through the long, curved surfaces of Monet's revolutionary paintings, which translate their literal horizontality into a figural verticality.

I have nothing but admiration for Giverny as a creation. But I feel that, when one visits it, the experience is frustrating, precisely because the disposition of space is not adjusted to the pace and progress of the walker, but is controlled by the painter's eye. In a sense, Monet has anticipated in his creation one of the essential relays of land art. Andy Goldsworthy is doing something similar when he arranges the intense colours of the natural world – for instance, yellow and red foliage – in order to make a vibrant Cibachrome print. For Goldsworthy, nature has become an inexhaustible source of ready-mades: the 'natural' element is selected with a view to its future appearance in an illustrated book, or a gallery display unit.

In referring to the system of the 'ready-made', I am at the same time invoking the acute analysis given by Thierry de Duve in his book, *Kant after Duchamp*.[2] Following the broad history of modern art from the time of Manet and the Impressionists, De Duve lays emphasis on the importance of the Salon as an institution hedged in by conventions and entry conditions, which are stoutly defended by the members of the Academy. As a result, he argues, there comes about a category of 'art in general' which emerges precisely to define the works which are not accepted by the Salon jury, and appear in public in the famous Salon des Refusés of 1863.

In De Duve's terms, Duchamp is at the same time exploiting and deconstructing this system when he submits to the Armoury Show 50 years later his famous *Fountain*, signed 'R. Mutt.' It is a matter of transgressing the specific limit which convention has traced between the art gallery and the world that is outside. What does it matter – we would now say – whether Duchamp created the *Fountain*, or his other 'ready-mades'?

The essential point is that he displaced an object and brought it within the distinctive circuit known as 'art'.

There can be little doubt that the exponents of land art are, to a great extent, working in relation to this system. Even an artist like David Nash, who sites his wooden totems in the faraway forests of the Lake District, is obliged to exhibit at the same time in museums and galleries. One of his most impressive works involved a transplant of a section of turf from the front of the Serpentine Gallery, in London, to the Welsh mountains, and a corresponding transplant which moved in the other direction, invading the trim turf of Hyde Park with its coarse and sturdy grasses. Though the material may indeed, in such a case, be living organic matter, the observance of the system of the 'ready-made' is still beyond question. What we observe in the gallery is not simply an object, but an object derived from a transgression of boundaries, which is ontologically *out of place.*

Perhaps it is Richard Long, among British land artists, who has most fully understood the stakes involved in land art, since he has always known precisely how to exploit the tension between the place of his practice (of his 'walk') and the place of exhibition. From the late 1960s onwards, in early works like the well-known *A Line Made by Walking*, he has managed to bring out the rhetorical disequilibrium between his gestures in the natural setting – always, as it were, innocent and transitory – and their semi-permanent registration in the context of the gallery work. This 'Line Made by Walking' is going to disappear in a few moments, but it is perpetuated by the image which we can view again and again, at our leisure. In a major key, compared to the minor key of the previous work, is Long's extraordinary *Allotment*, involving the dumping of many tons of chalky stone on the massive floor of an old factory in Liverpool – so that a high viewpoint was strictly necessary for the viewing of its geometrical regularities. In both cases, however, the specific way in which Long utilises the ready-made system is by creating a *mise-en-abîme* of perspective: by inscribing on a flat surface the fleeing lines which are the trace of the walker's experience of space.

Long also completed a discreet earthwork in the woods of the Villa Celle, in Tuscany, which balances the assertive presence of his green stone circle in the interior space of the *Fattoria* of the villa. This unique 'sculpture park', is at the same time an amalgam of olive-groves, 18th-century terraces and a 19th-century garden in the English style. Celle is specially interesting as initially, and in the areas adjoining the villa, it did indeed operate as a 'sculpture park' in the limited sense of the term: that is to say, sculptural works were placed regularly in an outdoor exhibition space which was conceived as a roofless gallery. Yet the further development of Celle – and above all the enlistment of artists who were able to complement the varied spatial settings of the park with their own advanced intuitions – led to much more ambitious effects. Some were still, in a sense, implicitly rejecting the natural surroundings in the very constraints which they imposed upon the visitor. For example, Robert Morris' intricately planned labyrinth – though splendidly made up of green and white marble derived from local quarries and reminiscent of local medieval churches – gave rise to a quality of experience very different from that obtained in the clipped yew labyrinths of the Renaissance garden. It is reputed that visitors who ventured to the centre of this structure on one occasion discovered a wildcat in the inmost chamber – which nicely illustrates the revenge of 'nature red in tooth and claw' on a minimalist incursion into her territory!

By contrast, the sculptor Richard Serra – always sensitive to the environment despite the fact that most of his works invade an already compromised urban setting – had the tact to place his work at Celle on the open face of a grassy hill, which his periodically placed stones help to reveal by establishing innumerable sequences and points of view. But it is perhaps the sculptor Dani Karavan who most economically and simply revives the spirit of the old English garden at Celle by using his construction simply to foreground the light and shade within the woodland area. Karavan's long lines of white concrete, which catch the light and allow it to be reflected off the adjacent moss-clad tree surfaces, are almost reminiscent of the little stone channels filled with running water which William Kent installed at Rousham in the 18th century, to light up the woodland paths with a reflection of the sky, and lead the visitor on in search of the next garden feature. Alone of the sculptors involved at Celle, Karavan seems to view his task as contributing to the syntax of the garden space, rather than simply installing a work in a natural setting.

The arrangement of works at Celle thus suggests a gamut of possibilities, at one end of which is the roofless gallery, stocked with sculptures which might as well be indoors, and at the other end of which is the installation which denies itself, so to speak, in bringing about the intensification of the garden experience. I would suggest that the same range can be demonstrated at some of the other notable sculpture parks in Europe, such as the Kröller-Müller Museum in Otterlo, where monumental works like Dubuffet's *Jardin d'émail* and Oldenburg's *Trowel* fight a heroic (but losing) battle against the natural environment, and at the same time occasional manifestations of a more discreet kind infiltrate and shape the experience of the landscape. There is no particular judgement of value implied here: simply the fact that the 'sculpture park' is an intersection between strategies that, for analytic purposes, should be seen as widely discrepant in their intentions and implications.

Both at Celle and at the Kröller-Müller, however, a visual expression of a different order is provided by the work of Ian Hamilton Finlay. In his case, it is not a question of simply contributing to the syntax of the garden space, let alone of planting sculptural works in outdoor exhibition areas. Instead, the desired object is a garden, a space symbolically invested with classical ideas and values as well as being a coherent and self-sufficient natural environment. In *Five Columns for the Kröller-Müller*, Finlay was able to revitalise a neglected but substantial area of the park, which was cleared of undergrowth, and formed a natural arena: the column bases added to the trunks of existing trees sacralised the space, and

Richard Long, A Line Made by Walking/England, *1967, framed work, 85x115.5 cm*

dedicated it to heroes implicated in the French Revolution, in the same way as English garden designers of the 18th century had commemorated the achievement of 'British Worthies'. At Celle, an ambitious initial project, involving a small classical temple and a pathway leading to a Virgilian grove, was modified, so that the latter feature only was carried out. But Finlay's grove amid the olive trees, utilising inscribed bronze tree-plaques and agricultural objects, still preserves its integrity and serves as an implicit critique on what occurs in the neighbouring 'Forest of the Avant-garde' (Finlay's title for the main section of the Celle sculpture park).

In order to gauge the full implications of Finlay's approach, it is important to take into account the time-scale of the garden – so different from the daily and seasonal routine of gallery space. His oldest single project, away from his home in Scotland, is the garden attached to the Max-Planck-Institut for Physics at Stuttgart, which has now developed to an extent where the dense foliage around the central pond appropriately complements the stone column installed there, and casts a shimmering light upon the lichen-encrusted surface of the inscription. Yet even the more recent and extensive garden at Stockwood Park, near Luton, which was completed in 1991, is beginning to show the dividends of the slow habituation of the garden features to their natural environment which is the gauge of the gardener's achievement. Finlay was fortunate, in this case, in being able to develop an area which retained many of the properties of an earlier garden, including fine mature trees and a sunken ha-ha. His own concern has been to build on this existing structure, and to overlay it with a network of allusive, inter-related features of his own.[3]

How does the garden, as I have begun to define it, fit into the current paradigms of contemporary art? The answer, in line with my earlier argument, must be that it proposes a totally different paradigm. There is no point in pretending that it can be understood in the context of the modernist ideologies which I have outlined, except to the extent that *de facto* (as in the case of Finlay's grove at Celle) the garden forms a critique of the other modes of annexing and referencing the natural world which have proliferated in the art of the post-war period. In this sense, the French landscape and garden designer, Bernard Lassus, is quite right to state that the garden is in itself an art form. It is not a receptacle for works of art, but a self-sufficient expression which, at the same time, has the distinctive role of manifesting the historical identity of a place in its concrete spatial relations. The 'Jardin des Retours' (Garden of Returns), which Lassus has been developing at Rochefort-sur-mer on the French Atlantic coast since 1983, is an unparalleled example of the imaginative challenge provided by this concept. Lassus was commissioned to work in an area which focused on the fine 17th-century industrial buildings of the Corderie Royale, which provided the rigging for French naval vessels. Instead of treating the building as a kind of château, and installing conventional parterres in the space opening up to the River Charente, he boldly determined to plan the river bank as a sequence of parallel walks, both formal and informal in their ground treatment, from which the facade of the main building could be viewed intermittently. At the same time, he introduced features reminiscent of the naval history of Rochefort, such as a wooden deck and mast with rigging built upon the remains of a German concrete blockhouse, and a line of palm-trees connoting the traffic in exotic plants between the port and the other parts of the world.

As a former student of Léger, who in the 1960s took part in the environmental experiments of the kinetic art movement, Lassus has brought an artist's training to a task which is today frequently entrusted to the landscape architect. It would be a great mistake to associate the practice of landscape architecture, in Britain or France, with the imaginative and recreative approach manifested by such exceptional garden designers as I have cited in this brief account. Equally, it would be wrong to minimise the contribution of such work to the overall renewal of categories of artistic expression which we are in the process of experiencing, now that the codes of Modernism are well on their way to becoming historicised.

Notes

1 Smithson's text, which originally appeared in *Artforum*, February 1993, was reprinted in *The Writings of Robert Smithson*, Nancy Holt (ed), New York University Press, New York, 1979, and published in a French translation in Gilles Tiberghien, *Land Art*, Art Data, Paris, 1993.

2 Thierry de Duve, *Kant after Duchamp*, MIT Press, Cambridge, Mass, 1996.

3 See my article, 'A Luton Arcadia: Ian Hamilton Finlay's Contribution to the English Neo-Classical Tradition', in *Journal of Garden History*, 13/1-2, pp104-12.

PIETY AND IMPIETY

The Little Spartan Wars

JOHN STATHATOS

It seems increasingly likely that once the millennial dust has settled, Ian Hamilton Finlay's garden at Stonypath will come to be recognised as one of the late 20th-century's most important artistic achievements. First hacked out of a barren Lanarkshire hillside by Finlay and his wife Sue more than 20 years ago, the garden consists of a complex and ever-expanding series of plantings, major landscape interventions, a succession of cunningly devised vistas and numerous three-dimensional artworks by Finlay and his collaborators. At the heart of Little Sparta lies the Garden Temple, around which building – its nature, identity and legal and cultural status – have raged the 'Little Spartan Wars'.

This is a conflict which has baffled many otherwise well-disposed observers, some of whom tend to treat it as an irrelevance, even at times an embarrassment. Others probably feel that it has dragged on long enough, that the point was made years ago, and that regularisation of the situation is now well overdue. Such an attitude, however, misinterprets an essential dimension of Finlay's principle creation: far from representing a rhetorical flourish, an entertaining side-show or a bloody-minded aberration, the Little Spartan Wars are an integral part of the Stonypath project. Ostensibly mired in abstruse legalistic arguments over local taxation, and superficially seen as yet another example of that ever-popular British spectator sport pitting plucky but eccentric Davids against the Goliaths of bureaucracy, they are in reality about *piety* and *impiety* and the meaning of these terms, if any, in the contemporary cultural arena.

For Finlay, the principal crisis of Western culture resides in the death of piety – in other words, in the commodification not only of culture, but of everything it ever stood for. Evidence of impiety may be found in the bureaucratic relegation of the arts under the rubric of 'recreation and leisure', in the way tradition is increasingly treated as external and, in the most literal sense, eccentric, and above all, perhaps, in the fact that public debate around such questions is no longer regarded as laudable or even permissible. For Finlay, the ongoing process of secularisation must be actively resisted, 'the garden consciously challenging the surrounding culture'. By this token, the artist's challenge to the bureaucrats of Strathclyde Region is not a piece of opportunistic street theatre but a reflection, albeit a partly symbolic one, of the principles espoused by the French revolutionaries commemorated in the garden's monuments and inscriptions.

The origins of the Little Spartan Wars are as undramatic and even banal as those of any other conflict. In October 1975, Sue Finlay applied for and received a 50 percent discretionary relief on the rateable value (property tax) relating to what was at the time described by Strathclyde Regional Council (SRC) as Stonypath Gallery, a converted barn in which Finlay displayed concrete poems and other collaborations published by the Wild Hawthorn Press. The relief was unilaterally withdrawn in December 1978 by the Region's Assistant Director of Finance on the grounds that 'such relief may not be granted to individuals, only to organisations'; two months later, a further communication added that the decision had been taken 'on the basis of the information provided which indicated that the premises were used to a large extent to house and display the work of an individual, and because access was by way of appointment thereby restricting public benefit'.

Finlay's response was matter-of-fact, refuting any suggestion that the Little Spartan conflict was deliberately provoked by him; this is clearly the retort of a man prepared to argue his case with bureaucracy, but oblivious of the fact that he is firing the opening salvo of a war now almost 20 years old:

Thank you for your letter in respect of our gallery discretionary rates relief. I would certainly like to appeal, and will be glad if you will tell me how I can do so. In respect of the 'terms of the scheme operated and approved by the Regional Council', I would assume – over-optimistically, as it may be – that 'terms' are to be interpreted in the light of a generous common sense, since our gallery is an aspect of culture and regional authorities, history shows, have not always been to the forefront in that area. I have never assumed any automatic rights to rates relief, but did assume that discussion would be permissible – would even be *desired* by the Region. In such discussion as I have had I have been given a number of very different reasons for the withdrawal of the relief – for example, *that if we were a proper gallery we would have an Arts Council grant*, and that *we are not an organisation*, and that *the public has restricted access to our gallery and garden, and that we might sell something* . . .

The question of public access, is, it seems to me, a crucial one. It is peculiarly dispiriting to have the 'appointment only' stipulation cited as if it were a *negative* stipulation. It is perfectly clear that all public access to anywhere is to some extent limited. (Try ringing your Rates

Dept. in Hamilton, at 6 am, for example). It is a fact that no serious visitor has ever been refused a visit to our gallery and garden, and the stipulation has been practical ... Thank you. I still hope we may be allowed an actual, serious discussion.

The conflict has been considerably complicated by Finlay's chronic agoraphobia, a condition which makes it impossible for him to leave Stonypath to attend trials or hearings; this factor, however, is balanced by his belief that debate about the nature of the temple and garden is in any case best conducted at Little Sparta itself, where the spell of the *genius loci* can manifest itself. Accordingly, Finlay was unable to attend an initial appeal scheduled for March 1979, proposing instead a meeting in the gallery, or else 'a proper phone discussion'. In the event, this discussion never took place, and, later that year, Finlay took the momentous step of re-designating Stonypath Gallery as a Garden Temple:

In any case your Rates demand is no longer applicable. We have clarified our position by re-defining our (one-time) gallery as a Temple, on the precedent of the Canova Temple (doubtless familiar to you) at Possagno. I look forward to hearing what the Strathclyde Region Rates Policy on Canova-type Temples presently is, and will of course be glad to welcome any official who cares to come and discuss this matter within temple hours.

On one level, Finlay is here as whole-heartedly serious as ever; but on another, the sheer malicious sense of fun with which he lobs this new ball at the Region is unmistakable. The correspondence which ensues is a minor work of art in itself:

Depute Assessor, Hamilton to Assistant Director of Finance, SRC, 22.5.80: I can think of no other description for the subject at Stonypath, Dunsyre than 'Art gallery'. It is used for the display of works of art, albeit that Mr. Finlay insists they are poems. Perhaps Mr. Finlay could suggest some tangible description for the subject to you, and I shall alter the description in the Valuation Roll.

HF to Assistant Director of Finance, SRC, 9.6.80: Thank you for your letter of 27 May. The correct description would be: Canova-type Garden Temple. I enclose the original Rates demand.

Depute Assessor, Hamilton to Assistant Director of Finance, SRC, 19.6.80: It seems that Mr. Hamilton Finlay

can suggest no normal description for the above subject and I am, therefore, not prepared to alter the existing Valuation Roll.

The dispute between Finlay and the various avatars of Strathclyde Regional Council is clearly as much one of language as of legalities, of style no less than substance: reading through these documents, it is immediately apparent that two different languages, two different ways of describing and ordering the world are here locked in conflict. The interlocutors may sometimes understand one another, they may even once in a while display sympathy for each other's position, but they represent essentially irreconcilable ideologies. Finlay's opponents are not brutes, and only rarely fools, but they remain incapable of breaking the administrative mould, that mind-state in which authority does not – *cannot* – debate, but only decree:

And again: to say that my work is that of an 'individual' is wholly ridiculous. What we have here is the expression, not of a person but of a *tradition*; actually and allegorically, every work is a collaboration. When Strathclyde quotes one as saying that the works are collaborations, *in order* to argue that they are the works of an individual, there is nothing to say – no Appeal to be made: they are not acknowledging any idea of exchange or discussion.

By November 1980, Strathclyde lost patience with Finlay and issued the first of a long string of Summary Warrants against him, warrants which it was clear the artist had no intention of complying with – or at least, not unless and until he was granted the opportunity of debating the issue on his own terms. One of the earliest and most concise formulations of Finlay's position regarding the status and nature of the Garden Temple is contained in an application for relief dated September 1981, under the section 'details of purposes for which property is used':

This building, correctly designated as a Garden Temple ... is properly part of the Stonypath garden and remains open to visitors throughout the year (even when the garden is dormant). It is widely recognised as a sanctuary, an integral part of a garden 'quite unlike any other', a 'philosophical garden' (Dr Stephen Bann); the purpose or aim of the temple is the traditional one of celebrating the Muses, and its contents are intimately related to the garden as (prosaically) an object and (ideally) a manifestation of the Western spiritual tradition. It is clear that education, literature, the fine arts, and religion, are not separable from this ideal.

In practice, there was little point in appealing to the Western spiritual tradition so far as the administrative machinery was concerned; Strathclyde's computer did not recognise the term 'garden temple', the Valuation & Rating (Scotland) Act 1956 took a singularly restrictive approach to the definition of temples, and, all in all, it was felt that to accommodate such eccentricity might open the floodgates to full-scale tax evasion by the inhabitants of Strathclyde. On an individual level, however, strange things sometimes happened which tended to reinforce Finlay's contention that the Garden Temple was possessed of a special character:

> The Sheriff Officer finally came – one chill dusk, in a very large silver car. He looked like Saint-Just. He told us of the dreadful things that would be done to us. All this was much as expected, and clearly no charade. In the temple, he embarked (in the office part) on an inventory (items to be carried away). Incredibly, the main part of the temple (once he entered it) seemed to lay him under a spell; he tore up the inventory, purchased a work, and paid the money due to Strathclyde *for* us (writing the cheque there and then).

This generous act could not, of course, stave off the Region's hounds forever, and a year later, a 'Schedule of Poinding', or summary warrant for the seizure of property, was served upon the Finlays, the bailiff's attentions being fixed most particularly upon 'a Porcelain Dryad representing Winter' and her two sisters in the garb of Autumn and Summer. By this time the stakes had also been raised by Finlay, who no longer sought *discretionary* relief on the Garden Temple, since this would leave its true status in limbo. The issue was now one of principle, and what Finlay demanded was *mandatory* rates relief, or at the very least the opportunity of presenting evidence in support of his claim to that effect. His response to an invitation from the Region to attend an appeal in respect of discretionary relief in December 1982 was headed, probably for the first time, by the phrase 'Little Spartan War':

> I refer to your letter of 3.12, which claims to refer to 'previous correspondence' and advises us that the Finance (Appeals) Sub-Committee 'have agreed to hear an appeal' by us 'in respect of discretionary rates for Little Sparta'.
>
> . . . To appeal for discretionary relief is to agree that we do not qualify for mandatory relief – which is (in turn) to agree that our description of the building (as a garden temple) is wrong. In short, you are offering us the opportunity to say we are wrong, this offer being camouflaged as an agreement to hear an appeal (which we have not asked for). This is very strategic but it is not acceptable here.
>
> What is needed – what has been needed for a long time – is a discussion, not artificially circumscribed by strategy or inflexibility, or by simple dimwittedness.

Tempers growing predictably shorter, the Scottish Arts Council (SAC) was invited to mediate, but despite a statutory duty to advise all Scottish government bodies on matters pertaining to the arts, could never quite bring itself to take a clear public line – a predictably pusillanimous position for which Finlay and, at times, others have castigated it. On 28 January 1983, the Chairman of the Region's Finance Committee advised the SAC Director that:

> While Mr. Finlay now appears to be claiming exemption for rates . . . for the premises initially described by him as a 'gallery' but now described by him as a 'Garden temple', it is this authority's view that he does not so qualify.
>
> . . . In accordance with the policy of the Regional Council, I, as Chairman of the Finance Committee, have authorised that the Sheriff Officer be allowed to carry out a sale and I am not prepared to rescind that order unless the outstanding rates, together with the statutory addition, are paid forthwith.

Two weeks later, in the presence of the irregular band of Finlay supporters known as Saint-Just Vigilantes and of several journalists, the Sheriff Officer from nearby Hamilton made an unsuccessful attempt to seize works from the Garden Temple in execution of Councillor Sanderson's decree. On this occasion, which became known as the First Battle of Little Sparta, he retired baffled, but returned a month later to make off with a number of objects; unfortunately, they turned out to be largely the property of an American museum, the Wadsworth Athenaeum in Connecticut, and after much huffing and puffing Strathclyde returned the lot in June 1988. According to a letter from the SRC Solicitor to the Scottish Legal Aid Board, 'said Sheriff Officer attempted to make arrangements for a Warrant sale, but without success as auctioneers were unwilling to be involved in view of Press interest in disputed claims to ownership by third parties'.

This concluded the more picturesque phase of the Little Spartan Wars, but despite the frequent intervention of distinguished artists, critics and academics from around the world, the Region continued its campaign of attrition. While the results were in the main as fruitless as those of the 1983 Budget Day Raid, the strain and anxiety caused by this intermittent persecution certainly left its mark on both Finlays. For a brief moment in 1985 it seemed as though the Region had decided, as much for the sake of its own reputation as anything else, to acquiesce in a change of status for the temple, but the proposed change was purely cosmetic:

> The garden temple has been declared a garden temple by the Regional Assessor. But the Region has immediately stated that it doesn't matter what it is called, the debt is to stand, and to multiply, (ie, the rates are to be demanded as before). The Sheriff Officer is concerned and wants to hire a Queen's Council, to defend us from him. Here we have several varieties of paradox.

In February 1988, the Region seized a substantial sum from the Finlays' account with the Bank of Scotland, but were forced to return part of it after further legal challenges. Later that year, the Region's Solicitor John H Wilson, who actually met with Finlay at Little Sparta and studied submissions from the Saint-Just Vigilantes, addressed the following letter to Finlay's solicitor:

> . . . what we are dealing with here is a question of interpretation of statute. It does not follow, because your client asserts the spirituality and religious nature of arts in general and neo-classicism in particular or because you or I understand the point they seek to make, that the provisions of Section 22(1) of the Valuation & Rating (Scotland) Act 1956 as amended automatically apply to the circumstances of this case. I do not think they can be applied.

This is an interesting document, inasmuch as it lucidly expounds the legal and philosophical differences between the parties. It also demonstrates the chasm separating them: to the Regional Solicitor's entirely reasonable (in terms of a legal and administrative discourse) point that 'it does not follow', Finlay would retort, with equal reason (in terms of a cultural and humanistic discourse) that it bloody well ought to follow. Wilson, clearly an exceptional and unusual civil servant, went on to recommend a Summary Trial as the best way of resolving the issue:

> There is . . . a fundamental difference of view on the law which is simply not capable of being resolved by meetings or correspondence; Only a Court can resolve the issue and a summary trial is a positive means to bring the issue to a conclusion; . . . Given the importance to Mr. Finlay of the principle he wishes to establish, as he de-scribed it to me at our meeting, it seems to me this is the only way out of the legal impasse.

Indeed, so convinced was the Regional Solicitor of the essential equity of this solution that he offered to pay the costs on both sides, including the hiring of senior council to represent Finlay. Sadly, this civilised proposal came to nothing in the end, due largely to Finlay's continuing ill-health and to pressing family problems.

Instead, during the course of a hearing held in early 1996 which hinged entirely on a minor procedural point of law, a motion entered on Finlay's behalf to have the Region's warrants set aside was defeated. No witnesses were called, nor was the case heard on the wider grounds of principle demanded by Finlay. As a result, the artist is once again liable to the Region for a considerable sum, Little Sparta is closed to the public, and the Garden Temple itself is no more, having been formally reclassified at Finlay's request as a storeroom, to which purpose it has now been put. The Scottish Arts Council continues to maintain that it cannot intervene in a legal dispute. For Finlay, who never nursed any illusions regarding the size of the windmills he has been tilting at, these facts are not unconnected:

> No doubt there is something absurd in expecting the Region or the SAC to aspire towards a single world in which, to cite an early poem by Stephen Spender, Death and Jerusalem would glorify also the crossing sweeper, but what else could socialism, Jacobinism, mean? Should interpretation of the law be exclusive of tradition and culture? We are asked to divide ourselves into parts and then to surrender the better parts without a struggle. This is surely ignominious.

A CIRCUMNAVIGATION OF LITTLE SPARTA
JOHN STATHATOS

Ian Hamilton Finlay, H/our Lady, *sundial, 1978, with Graeme Murray and Ron Costley (1983)*

Lochan Eck and the Saint Just Column *(1983)*

Ian Hamilton Finlay, USS Nautilus, *1979, with John Andrew (1981)*

Ian Hamilton Finlay, Obelisk, Upper Pool, 1982, with Nicholas Sloan (1983)

Ian Hamilton Finlay, The Goose Hut, *1982, with Andrew Townsend (1983)*

Ian Hamilton Finlay, Last Cruise of the Emden, *heroic emblem in stone, with John Andrew (1984)*

Ian Hamilton Finlay, Homage to the Villa d'Este, *aircraft carrier bird-table, 1972 (1981)*

Ian Hamilton Finlay, Be in Time, *wooden sundial, with John R Thorpe (1981)*

Ian Hamilton Finlay, Pretty, *cast slabs, with Jud Fine (1981)*

THE RENEWAL OF FRENCH GARDENING

JEAN-PIERRE LE DANTEC

A few years ago, I claimed that the art of gardens, in France, had almost disappeared with the apogee of modernity.[1] Although this seemed to be a polemical statement, it was more realistic than the prophesies of the 'death of art' in vogue around that time. The conditions for creating an art of gardens have themselves become so fragile in the 20th century, that this art is confronted ever more seriously with its demise. The lack of private commissions, the development of urban planning dealing purely with 'green spaces', the loss of knowledge and the forgetting of history, together with endless production of academic formulae, have all contributed to the crisis in garden landscaping as an art form.

Yet since the 1960s, the critique of the tenets of the International Style has allowed for the reemergence of thinking about landscape. Urbanism was seen by the Situationists, for example, as a technique of spatial banalisation participating in the society of the spectacle,[2] while the naturalism and objectivism of so-called planners and decision-makers, which denies that landscape is a cultural creation (in terms of it being both a physical reality shaped by craft and technique, and a phenomenon involving intentionality, culture and the viewer's unconscious) has been refuted by many artists and theoreticians.[3]

In France, a commitment to the spirit of place has recently been re-established by a new generation of landscape artists, led by Jacques Simon, Michel Corajoud and Jacques Sgard, who have established the Ecole du Paysage at Versailles; while Bernard Lassus' research into the field of 'landscape inhabitants'[4] has helped promote a modern theory of the landscape, revitalising the ideas developed by such people as Whately, Gilpin and the Marquis de Girardin in the 18th century. An ecological sensibility has also paved the way, so that interest in garden art and landscaping, once confined to a group of specialists, now attracts people on a far wider scale, who are anxious to maintain contact with nature in this increasingly urbanised world.

The beginning of the 1980s saw the emergence in France of a public commissions programme that advocated the creation and development of urban gardens. The Parc de la Villette in Paris, with its masterplan by the architect Bernard Tschumi, thus became the first of President Mitterrand's 'grands projects'. But La Villette also triggered a whole series of commissions in other cities, including Lyon and Lille, as well as in smaller towns, for example in Terrasson, that broke away from the typical 'green urban spaces' and the neo-'Alphadian'[5]

academicism that held sway in the park designs of the 1970s in Paris (for example at Les Halles, Georges Brassens and Belleville parks). The enthusiasm for innovation was further witnessed in the highly successful Chaumont-sur-Loire Garden Festival which, instead of being a dry, academic event, actually served to promote experimentation and international openness.

But that's not to say that the garden and landscape scene is in any way perfect. If we consider that the aim of the art of gardens and landscaping is to offer to our senses a kind of spatial narrative that can show us an ideal vision of man and nature, we might begin to see the difficulties that this good intention comes up against, both in France and elsewhere. For many of us, what we refer to as 'nature' is both limitless and vague: not only can the term apply to anything from quarks to the galaxies, as well as to the world we live in; but also 'nature's' very existence is itself in question in a world of science, technology and megalopolitan urbanisation that generates chaotic sprawling 'landscapes', via real and virtual communications networks.[6] On the other hand, science has taught us that the classical distinction of man and nature is no longer valid. The physics of 'matter-space-time', biology, and ecology have recognised man's place in the world as problematic, having seen that man does not conform to the role postulated by Descartes and Newton – man as an independent observer with the God-given quality of master and possessor of nature. Meanwhile Freudian discoveries, and the 20th century's own tragic history have shown even further that the idea of man driven by reason, progress and humanism (as exemplified in the gardens of Colonna and Burle-Marx, Le Nôtre and 'Capability' Brown) is actually based on a series of illusions.

All of the above might help to explain why it might be naive, in this era of 'supermodernity' to search for the art of gardens and landscaping,[7] that could restore the link with a tradition which never should have been broken – as if the crisis of modernist architecture and urban space had simply been a minor aberration. It also serves to show why garden and landscape art raises so many different problems. I would like to run through some of the contrasting ways designers have approached the subject, and show some examples, not in order to list or classify the work (as most of the designers cited below cannot really be categorised and may even apply to more than one category), but to highlight some central themes.

The debate continues between formalism and naturalism,

Bernard Lassus, LEFT FROM ABOVE: Le Labyrinthe des batailles navales, Jardin des Retours, Rochefort-sur-Mer, 1992, drawing; Crazannes, 1996, drawing; Passerelle d'Istres 'le serpent et les papillons', 1981, with drawing; RIGHT FROM ABOVE: Les Buissons optiques, Niort, 1993; Nîmes-Caissargues 1990; Uckange, 1980

albeit using new terminology, contrasting the neo arcadian landscaping to the resolute geometricism of neo-rationalism, deconstructivism and minimalism. Bernard Lassus, for example (in both his 'Jardin des Retours' in Rochefort-sur-Mer and in his projects on motorway developments), has subtly advocated the weaving of signs and symbols to evoke poetically the history and geography of a place and its intervention, the transformations in the world resulting from modernity and the resulting tangible changes. At the opposite end of the spectrum we find a designer such as Bernard Tschumi who, taking Barthes, Deleuze and Derrida as his points of reference, has designed a conceptual park at La Villette using a rectangular framework that is indifferent to its site. Punctuating the site with neo-Constructivist architectural *folies*, he has inserted a promenade running down the length of the park, and included thematic gardens conceived according to cinematic paradigms. But there are others too who are less involved in theory, including Michel Carajoud, creator of Parc du Sausset, or Jacques Sgard with his Parc André Malraux in Nanterre, who have applied themselves to studying and revealing the potential landscaping qualities of a site from their own interventions, which employ an undogmatic use of planting and geometry. Other designers, such as Alexandre Chemetoff (with his Jardin des Bambous at La Villette and Place de la Bourse in Lyon), and Henri Bava with Agence Ter (and their landscape designs at the Lycée Philippe Lamour in Nîmes), enjoy mixing both approaches although programmatic demands sometimes act as constraints; (Louis Benech and Pascal Cribier's restoration of the Tuileries gardens in Paris being a case in point).

The lessons of land art and the increasing number of sculptural installations, whether temporary or permanent, have shaken up the conventional concept of garden and landscape art by introducing new themes: *representation* (with the ambiguity between the real work and its written, drawn or photographed traces); *perception* (with new ways of seeing, for example through a high-speed train or car speeding through the landscape, or an aerial view); the *definition of landscapes* themselves (to include new types such as commercial areas with their garish advertising hoardings, or dead industrial estates); the *interventions* able to bring these themes to light and generate a debate; and the question of *planting* in these interventions. Jacques Simon's explorations are an example in this category; his work includes a floating 'forest' on the Seine, and a 'European flag' (seen from an aerial view only) of cornflowers and marigolds on a 20-hectare site. Michel Desvignes' work also explores and refers to land art in a highly sensitive and conceptual way, for example, with his landscaped courtyard for the rue de Meaux building designed by Renzo Piano in Paris, his 'cascade' garden for the 1993 Chaumont Festival; and his work at the place des Terreaux in Lyons.

The emergence of the ecological movement in all its manifestations (scholarly, ideological and political) will henceforth

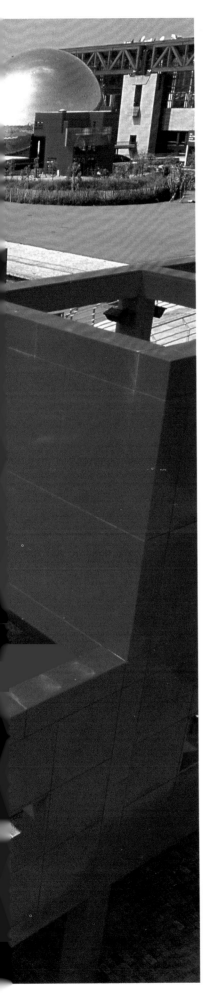

Parc de la Villette, Paris, OPPOSITE: Bernard Tschumi, folly (photo Arnauld Legrain/EPPGHY); FROM ABOVE: Bernard Tschumi, folly (F-Xavier Bouchart/EPPGHY); general view (photo Serge Delcroix/ EPPGHY); Alexandre Chemetoff, Jardin des bambous (photo Bogdan Konopka/EPPGHY)

impact upon every kind of garden and landscape art. In this era of globalisation, every stand taken by an artist on a site becomes by definition an ecological standpoint. This is why some designers or theoreticians, whilst advocating a return to the garden, mistrust this notion in so far as it implies a conventional distinction between cultured plantings and wild vegetation that is regarded as 'bad'. For instance, Alain Richert has proposed a simple 'soil garden' in Paris, as the basis of ultimate luxury in an urban universe dominated by mineral and the anti-natural elements. Gilles Clément, meanwhile, has for several years been developing his theory and practice of the 'garden in movement': having experimented in his own garden he has been able to give greater importance to (in an increasing number of more refined creations, such as the eastern section of Parc André Citroën and the park at La Défense in Paris, his park at Euralille, and his Rayol garden-conservatory in Provence) the concept of the garden as fallow land 'controlled' by spontaneous vegetation.

It remains to be seen, however, whether this rich variety of garden and landscape art (of which this article can only give a cursory presentation) will be a swan song or, instead, the prelude to a long-lasting renaissance of the art of gardens in France. Nevertheless we should bear in mind a point raised by Gilles Clément in the context of the 'planetary garden': in an era of 'widespread urbanity', it is less a matter of creating gardens as 'compositions of landscapes' in the 18th-century fashion, than of treating the earth itself, and its diverse landscapes, as an enormous domesticated garden. Approached this way, garden and landscape art can and will offer new and challenging possibilities.

Notes

1 Jean-Pierre Le Dantec, *Reading the French Garden*, MIT Press, Cambridge, Mass, 1990; first published Paris, 1987.

2 Theses 165-79 of *Society of the Spectacle*, Paris, 1967.

3 See Alain Roger, *La Théorie du paysage en France (1794–1994)*, Seyssel, 1995 and Jean-Pierre Le Dantec, *Jardins et Paysages*, Paris, 1996.

4 See *Jardins imaginaires,* Presses de la Renaissance, Paris, 1977.

5 Assistant to Haussmann, planner of the Parisian boulevards, and Prefect of Paris until the late 1880s, Adolphe Alphand developed a system of public gardens in Paris adopting a 'landscape style', itself invented by the landscape gardener Barillet-Deschamps, which remained dominant in Paris for over a century.

6 A phenomenon that I term 'widespread urbanity' in contrast to the city as such.

7 I have borrowed this concept from the anthropologist Marc Augé; see his *Non-Places: Introduction to an Anthropology of Supermodernity*, John Howe, trans, Verso, London, 1995; first published Paris, 1992.

8 The term comes from the Marquis de Girardin's superb treatise, *De la composition des paysages*, published 1777.

OPPOSITE: Michel Desvigne, landscaped inner courtyard, 1990, square des Bouleaux, rue de Meaux, Paris (architect Renzo Piano); Pascal Cribier, FROM ABOVE L TO R: Le Grand Carré, Jardin des Tuileries, Paris, started in 1992; Harras de la Sens, Rochefort-en-Yvelines, 1994; Jardin des Carrés, Limésy, Seine Maritime, 1989; Donjon de Vez, Vaumoise, 1992

BEYOND EDEN

The Art of the Garden or Art in the Garden

SUSANNE PRINZ

It is only natural that today while we view the great parks like the Bayreuth Hermitage, along with the gardens at Würlitz, Oranienbaum and Mosigkau as finished works of art, as *Gesamtkunstwerke*, we ignore the fact that contemporary parks are not usually graced with that designation. Similarly, we label the creator of the contemporary park not as a 'garden artist' but a 'landscape architect', and thereby place the garden in the realms of technology and science and not in the realms of art. Although we may have always judged the success of a finished product on aesthetic grounds, the garden has only recently won back its place in the world of art – a development that has emerged in view of certain contemporary crises, such as in the environment, that could no longer be ignored and via a resulting interest in ecology and sociology. Landscape is a social construct both in concept and reality and has recently become the subject of much cultural-philosophical debate.[1] There is a realisation that nature can be valued for the recreation it affords, as well as being an ideal political goal and an ennobling seal for every great popular project. This together with its plasticity has led to demands from both artists and scientists for landscaping that fits the times; landscaping which can be put to the test in the park – the place where man is least able to hide the truth from himself. It is in the park, rather than in what he imagines (against his better knowledge) to be the freedom of the 'natural' landscape, that man thinks of himself most as a social being.

Towards the end of the 1960s in the USA, artists like Robert Smithson, Richard Long, Walter de Maria and Richard Fleischner turned the public's attention to the landscape, by abandoning the museums and galleries that had been the official mediators of art and creating monumental sculpture within and with nature. In Germany the exhibition 'Skulpturenprojekt', curated in Münster (Westphalia) by Kaspar König, caused a mass exodus of art out of the art institutions. At the time it was the sociological perspective that dominated the debate over the function of public art. Consequently, in Germany, discussion on the relationship of art and nature did not develop much along formal-aesthetic lines, and neither did it immediately focus on landscape as the model for artistic reflection. Much more important was an interest in the man-made landscapes of Europe, cultivated over thousands of years. Many exhibitions were put on in parks and gardens, and new concepts of the museum were developed. The exhibition at Hombroich Island, for example, set out to enable the public to experience art in new ways, both inside and out, by developing the

museum as a type of cultural recreation centre, making art more convivial and inviting and building on the communicative qualities of art and nature. Since the beginning of the 1980s, when the influential documenta in Kassel made the Karlsauen one of the most important international exhibition spaces, artistic and philosophical debate on the garden and landscape architecture has intensified, so that the young French philosopher Philippe Nys can with some justification speak of a new *furor hortensis*.[2]

In the meantime the 'stage-managed' landscape has developed into a lucrative line of business in the public sector. Pseudo-countrified spaces in the middle of the city and playful, post-modern reconfigurations are beginning to re-enchant the world. At the same time artists are trying to find a meaningful way of reviving a historic art form – that of landscape gardening – in the contemporary context. As Udo Weilacher states, no 'hard and fast rules, not even a recognised language' have been laid down for these investigations into this border zone between fine art and landscape architecture.[3] Silvio Viette is somewhat more critical of the development, 'Conceptually, the aesthetic hermeneutics at the end of the 20th century have gone no further than Romanticism.'[4] And indeed, it seems as if most of today's projects that have anything to do with the park are a somewhat diffuse mix of primitivist and Romantic tendencies. Art and nature are forced into a model of mediation and reconciliation that aims to construct a harmony between them via a subjective nexus of meanings. An archetypal promise of salvation seems to be tied up with the very idea of 'garden'. More than ever before, the garden has to fulfil the individual's requirements of repose and peace, just as much as it has to meet the public good. It is clearly the last remaining place where nature and culture, work and pleasure, dynamic growth and cyclical renewal do not come into inextricable contradiction. In this sphere, the artist takes on the role of the free independent individual who figures as the counterimage to the 'man in the street' who is constrained by circumstances.

Artists attempt to meet the high expectation society places on them as soon as they take up work within and with nature in radically different ways. The best-known variant is probably that tendency in contemporary art (vaguely grouped under the name earth art) which in both its repertory of forms and its use of materials functions within the framework of nature. Situated outside the classical museum context, this type bore its best fruit in remote, lonely areas. Its archaic repertory of forms brings it close to land art from which it is sometimes hard to distinguish. In this category can be included, for example, Bruni and Barbarit's *Upwards Staircase* situated in an abandoned open-cast mine at Greifenhain, near Cottbus (Brandenburg). The painstakingly hand-constructed staircase brings together many different layers of meaning. On the one hand, by emphasising its overtly manual methods of construction, it draws attention to the labour that for decades was carried out on the site, and thereby gives that labour a new dignity. On the other hand, the staircase, which links a small clump of trees down in the open mine to a hill of brown coal at its upper edge, can be interpreted on a symbolic level. It can stand as a reminder of the origins of coal in the pre-Ice Age forests, as well as mankind's progress at the cost of environmental destruction. Bruni and Barbarit's work concerns itself with the extreme exploitation of human and natural resources without, however, ever denouncing it outright. It changes the way we look at the landscape by engaging with the region's collective memory.

Since 1991 the Biennale of European Land Art, Object Art and Multimedia (in which framework Bruni and Barbarit's work grew) has been consciously based on this long-forgotten, identity-forming role of the man-made landscape [*Kulturlandschaft*]. In the crisis-ridden *Länder,* several other initiatives and projects have attempted to fashion a strong sense of regional identity that is not wholly grounded in the cultural achievements of the past, by means of a symbiosis of contemporary art and nature.

The concept of remembrance, whether it is in the shape of a post-modern appropriation of form or of a direct confrontation with the collective historical memory of the target audience, offers some interesting solutions to that other difficult German theme – the two world wars and the commemoration of the victims who died in them. In particular, the use of inscriptions and emblematic images, which has been a characteristic of the public gardens of almost every epoch, seen from the viewpoint of the transmission of collective memories, seems to have found a contemporary language.

In 1987 at the second Münster Skulpturenprojekt the American artist Jenny Holzer who has been working with the medium of language for over 20 years, had five classical sandstone park benches set up around a war memorial in Münster castle gardens. The benches belong to her *Under a Rock* series (begun 1986), which deals with the causes and effects of war. One inscription read:

THE SOLDIERS SHOOT THE WOMEN RUNNING AND

THE CHILDREN SNEAKING. THEY CHASE DOWN GIRLS WHO DUCK IN RAVINES. THEY ADD LAND FOR YOU AND SOMETIMES PLEASE THEMSELVES. WHEN MEN ARE DEAD THEY ARE NOT SOLDIERS. BEFORE AND AFTER SOLDIERS DIE PEOPLE START SOBBING. SOLDIERS MUST DIE IMMEDIATELY TO SPARE YOU.[5]

These inscriptions seemed far more shocking in their bluntness than the nearby memorial, which is of the realistic type of 'Faithful soldier keeps watch over his dead comrades'. Strangely the sculpture, which can be directly experienced, is far less moving than the more abstract, linguistic message of Holzer's text. It seems that at the end of the development that began in the Enlightenment, which increasingly severed the word from the object, a statement about something is stronger than its concrete depiction.[6]

Holzer's analysis of the theme of war has continued and her installations have taken place in a wide variety of places. However, she has repeatedly returned to the park. It is there that death holds a traditional place, as Erwin Panofsky showed in his now classic study of Poussin's *Et in Arcadia Ego.*[7] None of the great 18th- and 19th-century parks turned their backs on this philosophical insight. Gardens like Wörlitz decked themselves out with exact replicas of the Isle des Peupliers in the park at Ermenonville, on which was situated the sarcophagus containing the mortal remains of Jean-Jacques Rousseau. Immediately beyond the so-called Elysian Fields at Stowe there is a still-consecrated church with a cemetery, and Prince Pückler-Muskau planned a funerary pyramid for himself and his wife within their lifetime in the grounds of the Branitzer Park. In our time we have chosen to allow both those political and philosophical meanings that these gardens undoubtedly possessed at the time of their creation to fall into neglect. They are judged in the light of aesthetics alone. In order to counteract this neglect and to bring these old truths to our attention, Holzer's artistic means are much more forceful than those used in the parks of the Enlightenment and the Romantic period which were reserved mostly for a highly educated audience.

In 1994 Holzer carried out a commission for a monument in the town of Nordhorn, in which she once again brought war and death into an association with nature. The installation *Black Garden* was added to an already existent memorial to the dead of both world wars. In an echo of the basic circular form of the park, Holzer laid out a series of concentric flowerbeds, broken only by paths and planted with only black flowers. In the middle was an apple tree of the variety called Arkansas

Black. An appropriate symbol for a garden of the dead in a deeply Christian region of Germany, the apple tree forges a link between the Fall and Salvation – traditionally the Tree of Knowledge (representing the Garden of Eden) was identified with an apple tree. The colour black, on the other hand, refers to death and consequently to Heaven. There is an unmistakable reference, too, in the bird's-eye perspective of the park as a target of vegetation, to the violent death of those mourned there. As in Münster, stone benches are provided with inscriptions. Here, however, Holzer is even more direct than she was ten years previously, describing various ways of dying in gruesome, graphic terms. One of the texts reads:

THE OCEAN WASHED THE DEAD. THEY ARE FACE UP FACE DOWN IN FOAM, BODIES ROLL FROM SWELLS TO OPEN IN THE MARSH.[8]

What is special about the small garden in Nordhorn is that, despite the unity and harmony that it achieves, allowing the visitor to reflect and contemplate in peace, not one of its constituent elements can be pinned down to one single meaning. Rather the elements are constantly interacting, and, according to the question that each visitor asks, narrate a different story about war and death.

The relative success of a garden – however that is to be understood and by whatever criteria it is judged on – seems to depend on its *narrative* quality, its ability to tell stories. The reason for this is probably that time is an important factor in the way we experience a garden. A garden has to be explored down to every nook and cranny, and can be experienced through contemplation only selectively at best. In this respect, it comes close to resembling theatre and literature, and draws

away from the fine arts, which depend above all on the contemplative gaze. That the language used to talk about the garden, at least under its aesthetic aspects, is primarily the language of painting is rooted in history. Even the word 'landscape', which is Dutch in origin, was originally used to designate views of nature and was only later transferred to the actual subjects of such pictures. And the picturesque, the ideal of every 'garden artist', arose out of pictorial appreciation. That pictures and gardens of that time convey comparable philosophical and political contents has unfortunately since been forgotten. The interrelation of the painterly and landscape gardening was increasingly reduced in Germany as almost everywhere else to vaguely pretty views, or at most views based on striking combinations of colour and form.

Walt Disney was alone in continuing to think narratively. However, that narrative can find a contemporary expression beyond the profit-oriented Technicolor dreams of Anaheim and Orlando is proved by some examples of recent years.

In 1994 an exhibition entitled *East of Eden* took place in the barely maintained rococo garden of Schloss Mosigkau, only a few kilometres from the Dessau Bauhaus. This brought together art from all over the world that revived in quite radically different ways the traditions of garden history. As well as a hedge-and-mirror labyrinth by the American conceptual artist Dan Graham and a bronze basket with the fruits of the French Revolution by the Scottish artist Ian Hamilton Finlay (both of whom never seem to be absent from any garden design of international standing), there were also works by artist who have previously concentrated on more traditional contexts. Sylvie Fleury's cadillac overgrown with roses, which replaced

FROM L TO R: Fortuyn/O'Brien, installation; Sylvie Fleury, installation, 'East of Eden', Schloss Mosigkau, Dessau, 1994

the former circular castle rosebed, belonged to a romantic pictorial tradition whose femininity has nothing to do with the austere German Romanticism that is epitomised in the pictorial language of Caspar David Friedrich. The symbolic aspect of traditional garden sculpture was addressed in an installation by Fortuyn/O'Brien. Small objects – bonsai, roots and tree stumps, modelled in bronze and Indian rubber – were dispersed in the nooks and crannies of an old garden maze and sprouted disconcertingly out of the urinals and waste pipes of the park's public toilets. Most obviously a metaphor for the natural life-cycle, the connections between these two half-public half-intimate spaces that seem to be evoked are nevertheless actually devoid of meaning. Even as the work's narrative content provides us with a bit of fun, it deliberately sidesteps meaning.

Margrund Smolka, whose cement sculpture is situated on an ABM (state job creation scheme) at Lehnin Lake not far from Berlin seduces us in a similar way to Fortuyn/O'Brien's piece. Even this so-called 'Lehnin Chair' is only secondly a symbol of nature under increasing threat from mankind. First of all, it is a site-specific sculpture that is also, in the modern sense of the word, autonomous.

The struggle to fuse art and nature into an indissoluble harmony, which for the German Romantics was in the end the moral benchmark of all things, was memorialised by Joseph Kosuth in his *Schiller Labyrinth*, which emerged at the time of the 175th anniversary of the University of Hohenheim bei Stuttgart. Situated in the inner courtyard of Hohenheim's former castle, Kosuth fulfils Novalis' dictum that, 'Nature will become moral, when She devotes herself to Art out of a true love of Art,

when she does what Art wills – Art, when it lives for and works according to Nature out of a true love for her' [*Die Natur wird moralisch seyn, wenn sie aus ächter Liebe zur Kunst – sich der Kunst hingiebt – thut, was die Kunst will – die Kunst, wenn sie aus ächter Liebe zur Natur – für die Natur lebt and nach der Natur arbeitet*].[9]

Man's obvious need to locate himself need not only be fulfilled by means of narrative monuments. Simple geometric forms and patterns have fulfilled this purpose since the days of Le Nôtre. 'Simple geometric forms, such as circles and squares, are familiar and memorable images. To understand the relationship of one space to another, one must first establish a sense of orientation in order to recognise new juxtapositions or changes. Simple geometries are, thus, best used in landscape architecture.'[10]

Over this basic structure of the garden, monuments, benches, pavilions and playgrounds overlay a second rhetorical level. Art's duty, then, is to enter into the mimetic and communicative routines of the social group that is to be confronted with the artwork in the sense of a cultural remembrance. The remembrance of things, which is art's traditional function and its transmitted iconographic content, can help art to do this. For it is things that reflect man back on himself: 'The world of things in which he lives has a time index, which points simultaneously to the present and to the various layers of the past.'[11]

In 1994 when Peter Walker designed a park and a corresponding atrium hall (with an artificial palm garden and a glass stand planted with artificial geraniums) for the new Munich airport, he was trying to create a space that allowed those arriving at the airport to orient themselves, whether they

FROM L TO R: Jenny Holzer, Black Garden, *1994, Nordhorn; Margrund Smolka,* Lehnin Chair, *1997, Lehnin Lake, Berlin*

were in a rush or whether they had all the time in the world. The formal modelling of the complex is based on a grid structure, which at once stands in relation to the architecture of the hotel and the whole airport complex, but which also reflects the former architectural use of the site. Box hedges, artificial grass and colourful gravel paths are used to organise the area. 'Oaktree' columns set up vertical accents. Critics accused Walker of having done no favours either to economy or ecology. And indeed Walter refuses to subject his conception of a communicative garden to any one ideological utopia. Rather, he came to the conclusion that since only very few people visit those gardens in remote areas, such gardens should come to people via the technical media, above all via photography. Geometric structures photograph particularly well. In the service of a true dialogue between man and garden, Walker forces man to dig deeper, and thereby to take the first step towards both art and nature.

A different aspect of the preoccupation with the relationship of humankind and nature in an age when each can be mechanically reproduced occurs in the work of Wolfgang Laib, whose pollen installations form poetic natural metaphors realised in the context of contemporary art. Since the 1950s, artists such as the German Tita Giese and the Americans Helen Mayer Harrison and Newton Harrison have come to a logical conclusion when faced with the increasingly evident ecological crisis and have exchanged the art institution for the public and open space. Tita Giese, for example, planned to fill the middle reservation of New York's Fifth Avenue with plants that were native to Manhattan before the European settlement. The Harrisons, whose works have been situated in areas directly effected by ecological crisis, returned to work within the museum, for example at the Kunst und Ausstellungshalle der Bundesrepublik Deutschland in 1996. On the roof of the collection they planted a large, luxuriant meadow of flowers, whose variety of species was to be found nowhere in nature. As well as providing a detailed classification of the species present and an indication of their rarity, this rooftop meadow brings nature into the artistic discourse. Nature was recognised as art in itself, something that was underlined through its integration into a public collection. An earlier example of this was Joseph Beuys' *700 Oak Trees* made for documenta 7.

The flora and fauna of an ancient landscape is also the starting point of of Lothar Baumgarten's work *The Big Patch of Grass* (*Das grosse Rasenstuck* 1996) at the Buchinger Clinic on Lake Constance. The work which covers 12 x 49 metres of wall space reflects the symbiosis of plants, animals and people formed in the surrounding area over thousands of years. Constituting a kind of mirror-image in words, 141 concepts evoke not only the images of the plants and animals themselves but penetrate deep into the local collective memory simply through the sound, the symbolic power inherent in the names, the hallowed vividness of the partly dialectical words and the arrangement of the concepts: 'pencils in the topography of nature: fish in the water, the birds in the sky, the mole in the earth, the hawk above the treeline.'[12]

Earlier in 1994 Lothar Baumgarten had already realised an actual garden for the Fondation Cartier in Paris, a work that is relevant to a discussion of the German art garden because it starts out from similar ideas to that of the Lake Constance work. The commission required a relatively small, pleasant,

FROM L TO R: Joseph Kosuth, Schiller Labyrinth, *1993; Peter Walker, garden of Kempinski Hotel, 1994, Munich*

triangular area surrounded on all sides by buildings and walls to be turned into a garden, and Baumgarten responded by developing a basic structure of simple geometric forms. The location of the garden's terrace was determined by means of inscribed circle. This established in turn the position of the oval-shaped depression which is sunk into the gently sloping site. The Fondation's museum building blocks the garden off from the road, but its glass construction sometimes affords uninterrupted views through to the garden and simultaneously reflects the garden image back on to itself. In addition, the glass walls fragment the light and 'transform the building into a crystal. The visitor's position is continuously questioned.'[13] Baumgarten took the crystal structure of the building into account on a symbolic level in his choice of his materials for the fountain and terrace. When planting out the garden, he chose native species that had largely vanished from urban Paris, and allowed them to grow in accordance with the prevailing light and soil conditions. In the Fondation Cartier garden, Baumgarten succeeded, as at Lake Constance, in bridging the gap between man, art and nature by taking advantage of the vast supply of cultural memories an area holds, though by using formally quite different means.

Notes

1 Cf Vietta, *Die vollendete Speculation führt zur Natur zurück*, Leipzig, 1995; Anne Cauquelin, *L'Invention du paysage*, Paris, 1989; *Le Débat*, vol 65, 1991; *Critique*, vol 577/578, 1995; more practically oriented is Udo Weilacher, *Zwischen Landschaft und Landart*, Berlin, 1996.

2 Philippe Nys, *Effervescences paysage*.

3 Weilacher, *Zwischen Landschaft...*, p41.

4 Vietta, *Die vollendete Speculation...*, p212.

5 *Skulpturenprojekte*, exhib cat, Münster, 1987, pp128-29.

6 It should be mentioned in qualification that this assessment is not universal. A contrary example might be the Vietnam War Memorial in Washington by Maya Lin. A few years ago this had to be supplemented by a realistic sculpture depicting three soldiers of differing rank and race, because veterans' groups did not feel properly represented by the memorial, although to judge by the numbers of visitors it was extremely successful with the wider public.

7 Erwin Panofsky, 'Et in Arcadia Ego: Poussin and the Elegaic Tradition', in *Meaning and the Visual Arts*, New York, 1955, pp295-320.

8 *The Black Garden*, cat, Nordhorn, 1994, pp58-59.

9 Novalis, *Allgemeinen Brouillon*, quoted in Vietta, *Die vollendete Speculation . . .*, p165.

10 Martha Scwartz, quoted without source in *Pages Paysages*, vol 4, p131.

11 Jan Assmann, *Das kulturelle Gedächtnis, Errinerung und politische Identität in frühen Hochkulture*, Munich, 1992, p20.

11 Lothar Baumgarten, accompanying text to the Buchinger Clinic, Überlingen, 1996.

12 Lothar Baumgarten, accompanying brochure for the Fondation Cartier, Paris, 1994.

Lothar Baumgarten, Theatrum Botanicum, *1994, Fondation Cartier pour l'Art Contemporain, Paris (photo Hervé Abadie)*

Arrangement of Local Stones, *1997, 36 boulders, 18.9x10.3 m, Morris Healy Gallery, New York*

NATURE WORKS
MEG WEBSTER

In the early 1980s I began making sculptural objects related to the body and installations intended to connect man to nature as a counter-action to nuclear proliferation and war. The objects were minimal and raw made from materials like soil, sand, hay, salt, contained water and moss. Large and often possible to enter physically, they acted as symbols for man's integration into the natural world and his safety within it. The viewer was required to exist as part of the world rather than regarding it as mere objective phenomena.

As I began working outside now making sculptures in the ground, I found a natural progression to gardened work. With the sculpture *Hollow* (1984-85) I needed to hold an almost vertical soil wall. At a garden centre buying red clover seed I discovered bulbs. Soon perennials were added. I thus made the bowl shaped interior a gardened space. When the work took on water during hard rains I discovered pumps, which became important in future works.

Hollow functioned as a raw, surprising object/building which a viewer discovers in a pastoral park landscape. The long walk down into the enclosed sunken earthen volume enhanced the work's symbolic charge. The flowering interior heightened delight and created a comforting wonder.

A similar work to *Hollow* called *Glen* (1988-89) was built at the Walker Art Center in Minneapolis. This time the interior garden wall was terraced, the walkway was shorter, made of steel and penetrated a high circular berm. The interior space was again an enclosed intimate space and cottage garden. A visitor experienced connection with the many flowering plants and the calm feeling of being within a secluded outdoor earthen room.

The plants acted as medium and fabric for the works. Stones and moving water became equally important as a medium. An installation named *Stream* (1992) was made in an open-air stepped courtyard at the Carnegie Museum in Pittsburgh. A large volume of water was pumped to the top level which then dropped down over stairs and terraces formed into streams and pools by large masses of local stones which had been lined with rubber.

With the work *Lifted Wetland* (1989) I held a natural wetland arrangement up to the viewer's gaze and bodily attention on a broad table-like structure. One could look into the wet, growing environment at close range. The importance of the wetland as an ecological structure was represented as well as the fact of how easy it is to create.

Along with wetlands I became interested in planting for wildlife. A permanent work called *Pass* (1991) was created at the Laumeier Sculpture Park in St Louis. Linked pools of water shaped like a bird and egg, rooms of fruit-bearing shrubs, plantings of pines and orchards, and a large sunken bowl planted with perennials created a field garden in a previously barren lawn. This work rambled. It speaks to the potential of land to make place as well as habitat. It was meant to be unmown. But the park authorities have not been able to go that far into natural landscaping.

A group of volunteer caretakers prune, weed and further the maintenance of this work. Neither the institution nor the caretakers have tried to call me. In fact with all my gardened works there has been an unexpected lack of desire for the owners or caretakers to communicate with me. It is as if the notions of installing unchanging steel or bronze sculpture is transferred into these gardened works. Even my queries are met with cool disinterest. I have decided that any further works made with gardened means will require a contract that agrees to bring me back periodically to the work for inclusion in its furthering.

The work called *Kitchen Garden* (1992) at the Contemporary Art Museum in Houston is a very good example of this. Problems were never brought to my attention. After creating the garden work and an extensive sculpture show inside, the museum may have worried about the expense of my additional visits. The work grew well providing a rich bed for raising vegetables, fruits, and native East Texas plants along the long ponds made to temper the hot climate. It was a wild and fervent environment in an otherwise manicured urban landscape. I was told much later some board members found the work offensive because of its wildness. The rubber pond liners were meant to be kept covered and mulched. The museum misunderstood this and allowed them to be exposed. This was the most distasteful aspect to some and one that could have been easily remedied. Nevertheless many people enjoyed the wild natural space. When the work was dismantled most of the plants were adopted and planted around the town.

Landscape customs are very established in America. Lawns must be mown. Hedges must be trimmed. Very little connection between the actual needs of bird, butterfly and insect are integrated into the ecologically sterile environment of urban and suburban American ground. Fear of snakes and insects certainly accounts for some of this, but identity and social status are factors as well. The need to control is coupled with the desire to extend the comfortable home environment onto the land. Native wild herbaceous plants and shrubs are relegated to roadsides. Anyone brave enough to allow their lawn to grow and the edges of their property to become thickets and hedgerows will most probably be fined. Herbicides, pesticides and overfertilisation often used to maintain the ubiquitous lawn are still not connected to rises in cancer and loss of species diversity. Shame is attached to a natural landscape. An aesthetic shift would allow significantly increased biological diversity to reemerge within our built environment.

Acoma Garden (1994-97) at the Denver Art Museum was successful in that volunteer gardeners adopted the work and have made it their own. I designed it with a central pond and upper pond. When the pump was turned on streams would reach every place in the work thus deep watering each plant in the dry climate of the high plains. The work was designed as a cottage garden to contrast with the highly organised annual plantings of the city park across the street. The gardeners have changed the water feature and made their own structural arrangements of plants thus altering some of the intention of my design. This is fine. The most important feature, that of informal intensive flower gardening of public space by the public, has been maintained and is indeed living well in the West.

A garden at a grammar school in Hartford, Connecticut has not reached this success as yet. It is designed as a teaching garden for young school children with many kinds of plants which encourage wildlife. Each classroom has its own geometrically shaped lawn surrounded by beds of flowers, shrubs and trees. Only two of the eight shaped lawns have been established and the little pond is roughed in. Several wild areas are growing well but leaving the institution with shame and embarrassment.

Signs will be created which describe the intent of the garden and speak about primary succession, the importance of wetland areas, as well as labelling all the plants. Edible and medicinal native plants can coexist in a vibrant landscape

FROM ABOVE: Stream, *1992, stone, rubber, pump, pipe, water, 14.1x37.7 m, Carnegie Museum, Pittsburgh, view from below; view of large pond from above*

with more highbred plants commonly used in landscaping. Thickets of tall grass, perennials and shrubs are important habitats of many creatures. Labels will speak of how each plant functions in the ecological system. A group of gardeners, students and teachers will be encouraged to participate in the caretaking, to continue the sign making, create an online website and extend the horticultural practices.

Several multisite urban garden projects have been designed although not yet built. They combine intensive food production, community gardening and allotments, demonstrations of ecological structures, as well as training in landscape and horticultural business practices. All these are combined with sculpturally shaped ground using underutilised parkland and vacant lots. These projects require extensive fundraising and community activation.

In my latest sculpture installation at the Morris Healy Gallery, New York, I have created a landscape with large boulders called *Arrangement of Local Stones* (1997). Like the informal plantings of the gardened works, the stones are organised as individuals. A different kind of order is created that is not architecturally or mathematically based. Each stone is presented for its own shape and characteristics. One wanders through the large stones sensing their beauty and experiencing their mass and tactility. It is natural space but organised with intent. A calm sense of place is presented. It is a stone strewn landscape which leads to a deeper room where a video showing twin lambs being born is running on an exposed video monitor. A waterfall video is projected. Large hand blown spheres of glass called *Largest Blown Sphere* engage the stones, reflect the flowing water and represent man's skill and care. The wall text, 'The soul pops and the lambs laugh loudly at ridiculous and irresponsible text' proposes the idea that humanity's successful caring and inhabitation of the planet would be served if old texts like the Book of Revelations or other equally damning promises were discredited. A culture who studies or integrates such texts will surely produce such things as nuclear war and ecological disaster. The tools of our brilliantly creative and caring production are all about us.

FROM ABOVE: Acoma Garden, *1994-97 plants, water, rubber, pump, brick, 28.3x37.7 m, Denver Art Museum, Denver, view of pond area after first season;* Glen, *1988-89, soil, plants, steel, 16.5 m diameter, Walker Arts Center, Minneapolis, people within the work after the plants have grown*

Lifted Wetland, *1989, wood, steel, pump, rubber, water, wetland plants,*
soil, stones, 7.5x11.3x2.3 m, Whitney Museum, New York